THE CHICAGO BULLS

An Illustrated Timeline

BY TAB BAMFORD

Reedy Press
PO Box 5131
St. Louis, MO 63139, USA
reedypress.com

Library of Congress Control Number: 2025936215

ISBN: 9781681065465

Cover and Interior Design: Craig Gartner with Linda Eckels

Front Cover Images: (*left to right*) Courtesy of Walter Iooss Jr./Sports Illustrated via Getty Images, courtesy of Focus On Sport/GettyImages, courtesy of Nathaniel S. Butler/NBAE via Getty Images, courtesy of Mike Ehrmann/Getty Images, (*bottom*) courtesy of Manny Milan/Sports Illustrated via Getty Images.
Back Cover Image: Courtesy of Nathaniel S. Butler/NBAE via Getty Images.
All interior images are courtesy of Getty Images unless otherwise noted.

Printed in Canada
25 26 27 28 29   5 4 3 2 1

DEDICATION

For my dad. I wish you were here to read this.

Coby White has excited Bulls fans since he arrived in 2019.

CONTENTS

ACKNOWLEDGMENTS

THIS BOOK WOULDN'T have been possible without my wife being an enormous help and my three boys continuously stirring my passion for sports. My friends throughout the years who have been huge basketball fans, Bulls season-ticket holders, and those who have engaged me in conversation about the game have all played a role in the production of this book.

There were plenty of reasons to enjoy a cigar for the Bulls in the 1990s.

The Worm was once hated in Chicago. When he arrived, the Bulls were almost unstoppable.

Michael Jordan the GOAT changed basketball in Chicago.

INTRODUCTION

SINCE 1966, THE NBA has had a team in Chicago. For the first 18 years of that team's existence, the Bulls didn't make many waves in the league. They had some star players and high draft picks, and they made postseason appearances, but Chicago never enjoyed a championship season.

In 1984, a young man from North Carolina arrived and changed the game in Chicago and around the world. Michael Jordan elevated the Chicago Bulls brand nationally, making their games must-see TV and their tickets must-haves for fans all over the country. In the 1990s, Jordan led the Bulls to the level of a dynasty the likes of which we hadn't seen in a generation. The Chicago Bulls were the most popular team in the world.

In the decades since Jordan left Chicago, the Bulls have enjoyed some remarkable performances and fun playoff runs. There have been some tremendous highs and devastating lows for the franchise and its fans, but Chicago has always supported its professional basketball team.

In this book, we'll go back to when it all began with Jerry Sloan and Johnny "Red" Kerr. We'll walk through the Norm Van Lier and Chet Walker years, enjoy the dominance of Artis Gilmore and the camera-loving days of Reggie Theus. We'll enjoy every game-altering performance from Jordan: the Slam Dunk Contests, MVPs, record-breaking numbers, and championships. We'll celebrate the contributions of Scottie Pippen, Horace Grant, Dennis Rodman, and Phil Jackson.

We'll look back at the Bulls having the No. 1 pick in the draft twice. We'll appreciate Derrick Rose's meteoric rise to stardom, and our hearts will break again with his fall. We'll look back fondly at the Chicago careers of Tyson Chandler, Kirk Hinrich, Luol Deng, Joakim Noah, Pau Gasol, and Jimmy Butler. And we'll enjoy the current team's accomplishments as well.

PHILA
21
PHILA
20
BULLS
5
PHILA
25
Wilson

THE BEGINNING

DICK KLEIN PLAYED professional basketball in Chicago and, after his on-court career ended and he transitioned to success in business, he bought the Chicago Packers (later Zephyrs). The Zephyrs moved to Baltimore and became the Bullets in 1963, but Klein was intent on having professional basketball in his adopted home town.

On January 16, 1966, the NBA awarded a franchise to Klein that became the Chicago Bulls. In their first season, the Bulls played their home games at the International Amphitheatre before moving to the Chicago Stadium, where they joined the more successful Chicago Blackhawks.

Klein was smart, and he brought home a local product who had starred in the NBA to be his first head coach: Johnny "Red" Kerr. He also acquired guards Jerry Sloan and Guy Rodgers in the expansion draft to lead his young team as they began play in the NBA.

With Kerr calling the shots, the Bulls became the only team in NBA history to qualify for the playoffs in their inaugural season. Sloan and Rodgers were named the Bulls' first two NBA All-Stars in the first season of the franchise's existence as well.

Bulls guard Guy Rogers (No. 5) tries to escape from Wilt Chamberlain and the Philadelphia 76ers defense as teammate George Wilson looks on.

JOHNNY "RED" KERR WINS COACH OF THE YEAR

When the Chicago Bulls took the court for the first time, a man familiar to basketball fans and suburban residents was sitting on the bench calling the shots. Johnny "Red" Kerr was the first head coach in the history of the franchise.

Kerr had led Tilden Technical High School to the 1950 Chicago Public League Championship before attending the University of Illinois and playing basketball there. Kerr remains one of the most successful players in Illini history, and he was named to the school's All-Century Team in 2004.

In the Bulls' first season, Kerr led the team to a somewhat surprising 33–48 record, which was good for fourth place in the Western Division and a playoff berth. For his influence on that result, Kerr was named the NBA's Coach of the Year. He was, of course, the first Bulls' coach to win the award because it was the franchise's first season.

In the Bulls' second season, Chicago finished 29–53 and in fourth place in the Western Division. The St. Louis Hawks, Los Angeles Lakers, and San Francisco Warriors placed ahead of the Bulls that season, with the top three teams all over .500 on the year.

The Bulls faced the Lakers in the first round of the 1968 playoffs. That Lakers team had a roster full of future Hall of Famers, led by Jerry West and Elgin Baylor. Chicago only managed to win Game 3 of the series as guard Flynn Robinson erupted for a game-high 41 points. LA won the series in five games.

Kerr served as the head coach of the Chicago Bulls for 163 regular-season games, winning 62 times. They won just one of eight postseason contests in his two seasons on the bench—the first two in franchise history.

Following the 1967–68 season, Kerr resigned his job as the head coach in Chicago. He was only 35 years old at the time, and immediately went to Phoenix to be the head coach of the Suns. He holds the unique distinction of being the first head coach in the history of both the Bulls and Suns organizations.

As a player, Kerr was an underrated big man. He was selected in the first round of the 1954 NBA Draft by the Syracuse Nationals. He appeared in 844 consecutive games from 1954 to 1965—an NBA record that would stand until Randy Smith broke it in 1983. He finished his playing career with more than 12,000 points and 10,000 rebounds and was an NBA All-Star three times (1956, 1959, and 1963).

Johnny "Red" Kerr was a local favorite and became the first head coach in the history of the Chicago Bulls.

In a battle of number 18s, Tom Boerwinkle defends Celtics forward and Hall of Famer Dave Cowens at the Boston Garden.

BIG TOM BOERWINKLE

NONE OF THE Bulls' draft picks in 1966 or 1967 spent more than the first three seasons of their respective careers in Chicago. The team needed an impact player to come from the draft; as a young organization, at some point the draft needed to help them build a roster.

The Bulls' third draft brought them the first player who would spend a significant amount of time wearing their jersey. With the fourth overall selection in the 1968 NBA Draft, the Bulls selected center Tom Boerwinkle out of the University of Tennessee.

Boerwinkle was a seven-foot center who had averaged a double-double in his final two seasons with the Volunteers. When he arrived in Chicago he joined a team that needed a big body inside who could clean up the glass—and he did precisely that.

Over his first four seasons, Boerwinkle averaged at least 11 rebounds per game and appeared in at least 80 contests per season. He was the perfect reliable big man the offense needed to support Jerry Sloan, Chet Walker, and Bob Love.

Injuries started affecting his play, limiting him to just eight games in the 1972–73 season and keeping him from playing at all during the 1977–78 campaign. But the Bulls' jersey was the only one Boerwinkle would wear in his 635-game career.

NOVEMBER 23
1968

BUTTERBEAN

ON NOVEMBER 23, 1968, the Bulls made a trade with their new rivals an hour north in Milwaukee. Chicago sent Flynn Robinson to the expansion Bucks for Bob Weiss and a forward named Bob Love.

In his two-plus NBA seasons before the trade, Love had never averaged more than seven points per game. In his first 35 games with the Bulls, Love averaged only 5.1 points per game. But the following year he exploded as a leader for the Bulls.

Over the 1969–70 and 1975–76 seasons, Love averaged 22.6 points and 7.1 rebounds per game. He was named an NBA All-Star in 1971, '72, and '73 and became the heartbeat of the team in Dick Motta's lineup.

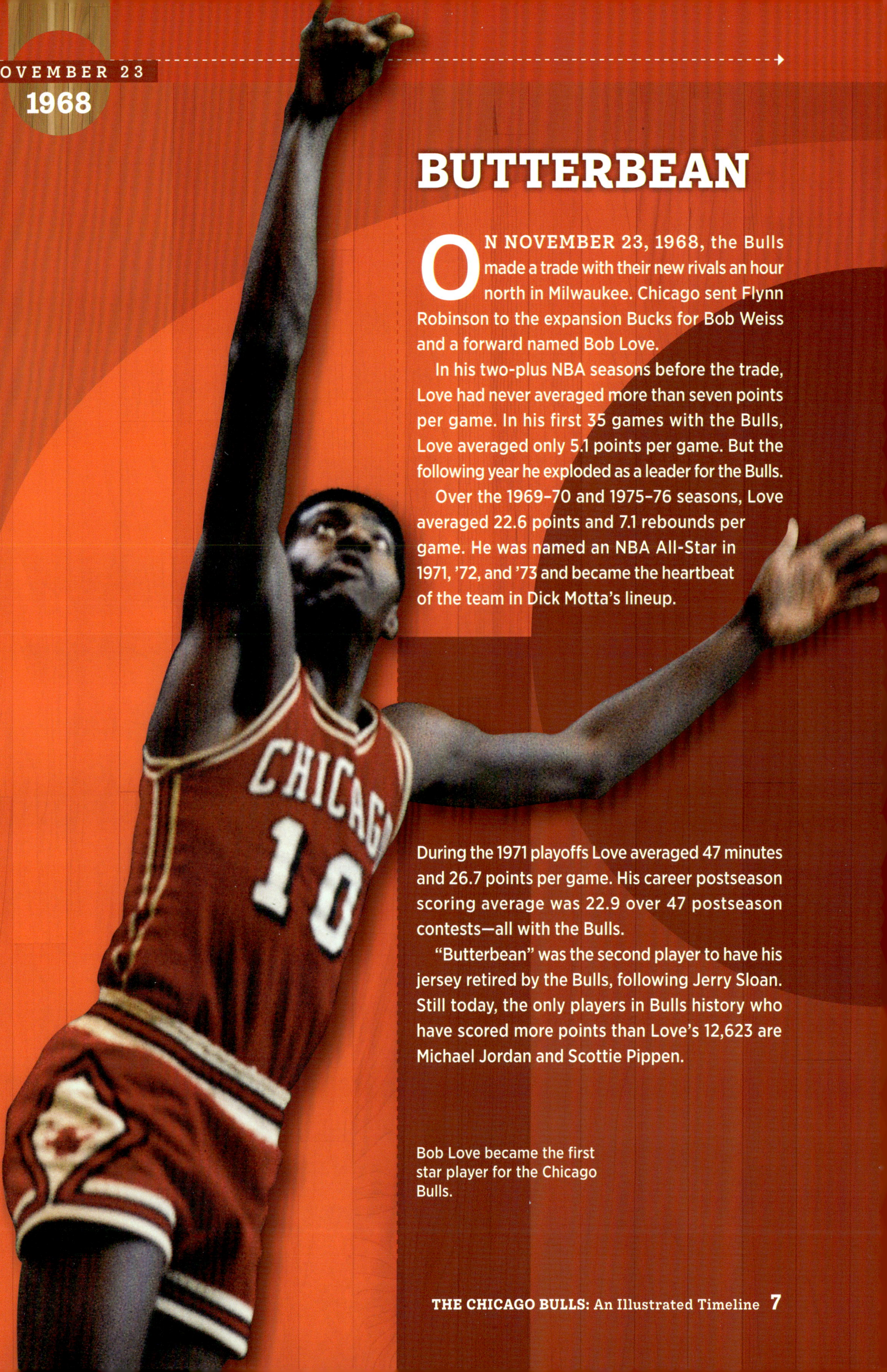

During the 1971 playoffs Love averaged 47 minutes and 26.7 points per game. His career postseason scoring average was 22.9 over 47 postseason contests—all with the Bulls.

"Butterbean" was the second player to have his jersey retired by the Bulls, following Jerry Sloan. Still today, the only players in Bulls history who have scored more points than Love's 12,623 are Michael Jordan and Scottie Pippen.

Bob Love became the first star player for the Chicago Bulls.

UFFALO
8
CHICAG

THE DRAFT

1969

STORMIN' NORMAN

NORM VAN LIER was one of the most popular Chicago Bulls of the 1970s, and he was arguably their first really good draft pick. Ironically, even though he was drafted by the Bulls, Van Lier didn't start his NBA career in Chicago.

The Bulls selected Van Lier 34th overall in the 1969 NBA Draft but immediately traded him to the Cincinnati Royals for Walt Wesley. Two years later the Bulls brought Van Lier back from Cincinnati, and he took over the backcourt for the next seven years.

Van Lier was an NBA All-Star for the Bulls during the 1973–74, 1975–76, and 1976–77 seasons, and he was named to three NBA All-Defense First Teams and five NBA All-Defense Second Teams during his career.

"Stormin' Norman" averaged 12.2 points, 6.9 assists, and 1.9 steals per game in 535 regular-season appearances for the Bulls during his career. In seven career postseason series with Chicago, Van Lier averaged 13.9 points, 5 rebounds, and 6.2 assists per game.

Van Lier's best season for the Bulls was the 1973–74 campaign, his first time as an All-Star selection. He averaged 14.3 points, 6.9 assists, and 4.7 rebounds that year and finished ninth in NBA MVP voting. That season was the first time he was named to the NBA's All-Defensive First Team and the highest he would finish in league MVP voting.

Van Lier was known as an aggressive defender who made life miserable for opponents. The Bulls' backcourt of Jerry Sloan and Van Lier was one of the best defensive guard pairs in the entire league. Van Lier's defense gained more league-wide recognition after he was credited with ten steals in Game Six of a playoff series against the Lakers in 1973. His three NBA All-Defense First Teams and five NBA All-Defense Second Teams selections are the most for a player who has not been inducted into the Naismith Basketball Hall of Fame.

He would receive votes for the Most Valuable Player Award after the following three seasons as well. His best scoring season for the Bulls was the 1974–75 season, in which he averaged 15.0 points per game. Van Lier also owned one NBA record for almost 25 years. Van Lier hit an 84-foot shot on January 19, 1977—the longest shot in the history of the league. That record stood until Baron Davis hit an 89-footer on November 17, 2001.

He was waived by the Bulls in October of 1978 and briefly played for the Milwaukee Bucks.

Van Lier ranks fourth in Bulls' history in assists (3,676) and fourth in steals (724). His 19,122 minutes played for the Bulls rank seventh in franchise history.

He returned to Chicago and worked as a color analyst on radio broadcasts from 1980 to 1982 and then did television work for Bulls games from 1992 to 2009. His energy on broadcasts was infectious, and he always told you exactly how he felt about the team's performance that night. Fans continued to love him while he was on the broadcasting side of the game. Sadly, he passed away on the same day as Johnny "Red" Kerr—February 25, 2009.

Many fans still feel today that Van Lier's No. 2 should be retired by the Bulls.

"Stormin' Norman" was beloved in Chicago on the court and behind the mic.

CHET THE JET

ON SEPTEMBER 2, 1969, the Bulls traded forward Jim Washington "home" to Philadelphia. Washington was born in Philly and attended Villanova before being selected with the eighth overall pick in the 1965 NBA Draft. He had averaged 11.4 points per game over three seasons with the Bulls.

In return for Washington and a player to be named later (Bob Kauffman), Chicago received a star: Chet Walker.

The Bradley University product had been an NBA All-Star in three of his seven seasons with the 76ers and won an NBA championship in 1967 before the trade. Over his six seasons in Chicago, Walker was named an All-Star four times—including in his first two seasons with the Bulls.

Walker's scoring average went up to over 21 points per game for his first three seasons in Chicago; he averaged over 20 per game over 474 games with the Bulls. Known as "Chet the Jet," he was lightning quick on the court.

Walker was inducted to the Naismith Memorial Basketball Hall of Fame—voted in by the Veterans Committee—in 2012.

Chet Walker was one of the first star scorers in Bulls history.

CALLING KC HOME?

EVEN THOUGH THE Bulls made the playoffs in their first season of existence, there were early struggles to garner interest in Chicago. The city showed up in droves for the Blackhawks and Bears, but the late 1960s weren't an easy time for basketball fans in the city.

On November 7, 1969, the Bulls reached an all-time low when they beat the Seattle SuperSonics in front of only 891 fans at the Chicago Stadium. That season the team scheduled eight home games in Kansas City in an effort to make money.

That season went better than expected, however. The Bulls won 39 games and made the playoffs. They started to attract more fans thanks to promotions that sprung from the mind of Pat Williams, who was hired away from the Philadelphia 76ers to serve as the general manager. He had been the business manager of the Sixers.

The Bulls played "home" games in Kansas City.

Chicago
53

ARTIS ARRIVES

IN 1971, FOR the first time, the Bulls drafted a player who would become a Hall of Famer. But he wouldn't join their lineup for five seasons.

Center Artis Gilmore lasted until the 117th overall pick in the 1971 NBA Draft. However, he was also selected by the Kentucky Colonels in the rival ABA draft that same year, and Gilmore opted to play for them to start his professional career.

Gilmore was terrific there, helping Kentucky win an ABA championship in 1975 and averaging 22.3 points and 11.9 rebounds per game. He was named All-ABA in all five of his seasons with the Colonels.

But the Bulls were able to select him again in the summer of 1976 in the dispersal draft. Finally in Chicago, he would spend the following six seasons establishing himself as a dominant big man in the NBA as well.

Between 1977 and 1982, "The A-Train" averaged 20.1 points, 11.5 rebounds, and 2.2 blocks per game for the Bulls. He also represented Chicago in the NBA All-Star Game four times in those six seasons.

In three playoff series for the Bulls in 1977 and 1981, Gilmore pulled down 106 rebounds in only nine games. He was magnificent in the Bulls' two-game sweep of the Knicks in the first round of the 1981 playoffs, scoring 38 points with 26 rebounds and nine blocks. In the second round, the Bulls were swept by the Celtics despite Gilmore scoring 70 with 40 rebounds in four games.

Gilmore remains the Bulls' all-time leader in blocked shots with 1,029—201 more than Michael Jordan, who ranks second. He also ranks in the top 10 all-time in offensive, defensive, and total rebounds and is the Bulls' all-time leader in field goal percentage (58.7).

Artis Gilmore became the first player drafted by the Chicago Bulls to be inducted into the Naismith Memorial Basketball Hall of Fame.

DICK MOTTA

Dick Motta was the second Bulls coach to be named the NBA's Coach of the Year.

WHEN JOHNNY KERR moved on from his head coaching duties in the summer of 1968, the Bulls turned to the college ranks for the second head coach in the history of the franchise. Dick Motta, who had been successful in four seasons at Wichita State, was brought in to take the franchise forward.

The first season Motta was in Chicago was tough; the Bulls won only 33 games and finished in fifth place. But the following season the Bulls made the playoffs, and that became a regular occurrence while he was the head coach.

Between the 1970–71 and 1973–74 seasons the Bulls won at least 50 games each year, and Motta was named the NBA Coach of the Year in 1971. Chicago finished second in the division for four straight years before winning the division with 47 wins in 1974–75. Motta led the Bulls to the Western Conference Finals in 1975, where they lost to the Golden State Warriors.

The bottom fell out in the 1976–77 season, however. Chicago won only 24 games and fell out of the playoffs for the first time in since Motta's first season as the head coach. When the season ended, Motta resigned and took the head coaching job with the Washington Bullets.

Today, Motta's 356 wins rank second in franchise history behind only Phil Jackson's 545.

1972

WIRTZ BUYS THE BULLS

IN 1972, THE Bulls were sold amid controversy. Founding owner Dick Klein had seen revenues decline enough that he decided it was time to get out of the basketball business. There were a few suitors ready to make an offer, but the team ended up selling to the owners of the Chicago Stadium—and the Chicago Blackhawks—Arthur Wirtz.

The sale made sense on the surface. The Bulls shared the stadium with the Blackhawks, after all. But Milwaukee real estate broker Marvin Fishman, who was one of the other potential buyers, believed there was dirty poker being played in the sale. Fishman filed an antitrust lawsuit, claiming Wirtz used his influence on the NBA and ownership of the stadium to force the decision by the league.

It took 10 years to finally settle the suit, and it cost Bulls ownership $12.5 million to make things square. By that time, Arthur Wirtz had passed away and his son, Bill, controlled the Bulls, the Blackhawks, and Chicago Stadium.

When the suit settled, Bill Wirtz said the team was in no way for sale. Of course, this came one week after the team had made the third overall pick in the 1984 NBA Draft . . . a young man from North Carolina who would wear No. 23 for the Bulls.

A year later, however, Wirtz would change his mind and move on from owning both tenants of the Chicago Stadium.

For a number of years, the Wirtz family owned but tenants at the Chicago Stadium—the Bulls and Blackhawks.

Walt Frazier dives for a ball away from Jerry West during the 1973 NBA All-Star Game at the Chicago Stadium.

CHICAGO HOSTS THE 1973 ALL-STAR GAME

IN THE MIDST of their struggles in the early 1970s, the Chicago Bulls hosted the 1973 NBA All-Star Game. It was the first time the franchise had hosted the event, and the game was loaded with future Hall of Famers.

Unfortunately, two of the NBA's biggest stars—Kareem Abdul-Jabbar and Rick Barry—did not play in the game. The Bulls were represented by Bob Love and Chet Walker, who scored six and four points, respectively, for the Western Conference in the game.

Nate "Tiny" Archibald led the West team with 17 points. The West roster also included Wilt Chamberlain, Jerry West, Bob Lanier, and Spencer Haywood, among others.

The Eastern Conference won the game 104–84. Boston's Dave Cowens, who led the East with 15 points and 13 rebounds, was named the game's Most Valuable Player. The East roster also included Walt "Clyde" Frazier, John Havlicek, "Pistol" Pete Maravich, Elvin Hayes, Wes Unseld, Lenny Wilkins, and Bill Bradley.

Bill Russell was in attendance—calling the game on ABC. Chicago wouldn't host another All-Star Game until 1988, and would only host the event twice in the Chicago Stadium.

MAY DAY

IN 1976 COLLEGE basketball was bigger than professional hoops in the US, and it was apparent that one team was the best in the land: the Indiana Hoosiers.

IU ran the table, winning an NCAA championship with an undefeated record. That team is still the last college team to finish the season without a blemish on its record. And one of the leaders of that team was forward Scott May. He averaged over 23 points per game and went on to star for the United States in the Olympics as well.

That summer, the Chicago Bulls held the highest draft pick in franchise history: No. 2 overall. There were some tempting names at the top of the draft, including Maryland guard John Lucas and Notre Dame wing Adrian Dantley. When Lucas's name was the first called, the Bulls selected May.

May was named to the NBA All-Rookie team after averaging 14.2 points in his first professional season. Unfortunately, injuries started to limit his availability, and the Bulls waived him after five seasons. After two more years of injuries, May went on to play in Italy for a number of years.

The Bulls selected Scott May second overall in the 1976 NBA Draft.

RIVERBOAT REGGIE

WITH THE NINTH pick in the 1978 NBA Draft, the Bulls selected UNLV guard Reggie Theus. "Riverboat Reggie" was a high-flying scorer who jumped into the lineup and made an immediate impact.

Theus was six-foot-seven and could play either guard position. He made the NBA's All-Rookie team and was the runner-up for the NBA Rookie of the Year Award in 1979 after he averaged 16.3 points and 5.2 assists per game. He was second on the team in scoring behind Artis Gilmore.

In his first two seasons in the league, Theus enjoyed some familiarity to start his career; his backcourt mate in Chicago was UNLV teammate Ricky Sobers.

Theus represented the Bulls in the 1981 and 1983 NBA All-Star Games. The 1982–83 season was his best in Chicago. Theus averaged a career-high 23.8 points per game and appeared in all 82 games.

His popularity wasn't only for his play on the court. His other nickname was "Rush Street Reggie" because he lived up the street from the Chicago Stadium and was frequently spotted enjoying the night life in Chicago.

Even with his rumored appreciation for the after-hours scene in Chicago, Theus appeared in all 82 games in each of his first five seasons in the NBA. And he averaged at least 34 minutes per night in his second through fifth seasons with the Bulls.

During the 1983–84 season, new head coach Kevin Loughery controversially decided to bench Theus in favor of rookies Mitchell Wiggins and Ennis Whatley. The Bulls won seven of their first eight games with Theus out of the lineup. The Bulls traded Theus to Kansas City on February 15, 1984.

Theus's time with the Bulls was tumultuous on and off the court. During his five-plus seasons in Chicago, Theus played for five different head coaches: Jerry Sloan, Phil Johnson, Rod Thorn, Paul Westhead, and Kevin Loughery.

The Bulls qualified for the playoffs just once during Theus's time in Chicago, following the 1980–81 season. The Bulls swept the Knicks in the first-round, best-of-three series with Theus scoring 37 points and dishing out 11 assists in the clinching victory.

Unfortunately, the Boston Celtics were waiting for the Bulls in the next round. The Larry Bird–led Celtics swept the Bulls 4–0 in that series, but Theus led Chicago in points (18.0 per game) and assists (5.5 per game) in the series.

Theus appeared in 441 regular-season games for the Bulls (332 starts) before he was dealt to Kansas City. He averaged 18.8 points per game for the Bulls, with his best offensive season coming in 1982–83 when he posted a career-high 23.8 point-per-game average. He was also a sound defender, averaging better than one steal per game in each of his five full seasons in Chicago.

He is one of 25 Chicago Bulls to make the NBA All-Rookie First Team, joining Phil Ford, Mychal Thompson, Ron Brewer, and Terry Tyler on the 1978–79 list.

Theus's personal life remained interesting after his playing career. He took up acting and broadcasting, appearing on the TV show *Hang Time* and making cameos in a number of feature films. His No. 23 was retired by UNLV in 1997. His son, Brennen Davis, was drafted by the Chicago Cubs in the second round of the 2018 MLB Draft; Davis has said Theus is not part of his life, however.

Theus still ranks among the Bulls' top 10 all-time in a number of statistical categories, including total points, assists, and steals.

Riverboat Reggie made headlines on and off the court in Chicago.

NBA

Jerry Sloan's number was the first in the rafters at the Chicago Stadium.

NO. 4 RETIRED

THE FIRST NUMBER to be retired by the Bulls and to go into the rafters at the Chicago Stadium was for a player selected in their expansion draft. Jerry Sloan had been one of the first stars for the franchise, so his number 4 being taken out of circulation on February 18, 1978, made all the sense in the world.

Sloan appeared in two NBA All-Star Games for the Bulls (1967, 1969), and he was named to the All-Defensive First Team four times and Second Team twice during his illustrious career in Chicago. The best season of his career was the 1970–71 campaign, when Sloan averaged 18.3 points and 8.8 rebounds per game, both career highs.

After appearing in 59 games as a rookie for Baltimore, he spent the final 696 games of his career in a Bulls jersey. Only three players—Jordan, Pippen and Hinrich—have appeared in more games for the Bulls to this day. He still ranks fifth in franchise history in points scored. He averaged 14.7 points, 7.7 rebounds, and 2.2 steals per game for the Bulls. (The NBA started tracking steals in the 1973–74 season when Sloan was already 31 years old.)

SLOAN TAKES OVER

Sloan speaking as the Bulls' head coach

HIS JERSEY WAS retired in February of 1978, but Jerry Sloan wasn't done with the Bulls organization. He served as an assistant coach during the 1977–78 season, and, on April 28, 1979, Sloan was named the Bulls' head coach.

The first season of Sloan's head coaching career was a tough one. In the wake of losing the coin flip for Magic Johnson at the 1979 NBA Draft, the Bulls won just 30 games. But the 37-year-old head coach was building a foundation for success.

The 1980–81 season saw the Bulls qualify for the postseason with 45 wins, led by Reggie Theus and Artis Gilmore. The Bulls eliminated the Knicks in the first round of the Eastern Conference playoffs, winning the first two games of the best-of-three series. They were swept by the Larry Bird–led Celtics in the second round, however.

Unfortunately, the Bulls level of play dropped off during the following season, when they won only 19 of their first 51 games. On February 17, 1982, the Bulls fired Sloan.

He moved on to serve as an assistant in Utah for three seasons and took over as the Jazz head coach in the middle of the 1988–89 season. Ironically, the furthest he ever advanced with a team was losing back-to-back NBA championships to the Bulls. He was inducted into the Naismith Memorial Basketball Hall of Fame as a coach.

1979

A NOT-SO-MAGIC COIN TOSS

David Greenwood was the Bulls' first pick in the 1979 NBA Draft.

THE 1979 NBA Draft changed the history of the NBA. It could have changed the history of the Chicago Bulls—if only Bulls General Manager Rod Thorn had called tails.

Back then, the top pick in the NBA draft was annually determined by a coin flip between the teams with the worst records in each conference. Injuries and a coaching change during the 1978–79 season led the Bulls to an Eastern Conference-worst 31–51 mark. They would get to pick heads or tails.

On the other side of the coin—literally—were the Los Angeles Lakers. The Lakers weren't bad at the time, but they owned the pick because free agent Gail Goodrich had signed with the New Orleans Jazz; the compensation for the free agent signing at the time was the Jazz transferring their pick to the Lakers.

Thorn called heads contrary to his usual habit. "Any time I had ever called anything myself with a coin, I always called tails," Thorn told NBA.com in 2018. "That was the ironic part of it."

Had Thorn stuck with his gut, the Bulls would have owned the top pick. And that pick was Magic Johnson, who went on to have an incredible, Hall of Fame career in LA. In his memoir years later, Johnson claimed he would have returned to Michigan State rather than play for the Bulls, but the possibilities of the LA market persuaded him to turn pro at the time.

Instead, the Bulls selected power forward Dave Greenwood from UCLA. He appeared in 464 games over six seasons with the Bulls. Greenwood made the All-Rookie team and averaged better than 16 points per game in his first season, but he wasn't Magic.

Imagine if Magic and Larry Bird had played against each other in the Eastern Conference for all those years instead of playing on opposite coasts of the country!

1981

ORLANDO TO CHICAGO

CHICAGO FANS WERE excited about the 1981 NBA Draft—but not necessarily because of the Bulls. The top two players in that year's draft were local products: DePaul University forward Mark Aguirre and Indiana University guard Isiah Thomas. And, sadly, the two would become teammates in Detroit during the Bad Boys era.

The Bulls owned the sixth overall pick in the first round that year thanks to a pick swap with the Atlanta Hawks, and they stayed relatively close to home with their selection. Chicago went with Notre Dame forward Orlando Woolridge.

Woolridge had shown the ability to score in South Bend, but he showed even more in the NBA. After averaging only 7.3 points per game as a rookie, his scoring average climbed into double figures and continued to increase in each of the following seasons in Chicago. He posted a career-best 22.9 points per game during the 1984–85 season.

Woolridge's tenure in Chicago ended when he signed with the New Jersey Nets in 1986; the Bulls received a collection of draft picks as compensation.

Woolridge took his scoring ability from South Bend to Chicago.

Corzine played seven seasons for the Bulls.

GILMORE FOR CORZINE

IN JULY OF 1982, the Bulls made the first controversial trade in the history of the franchise. All-Star center Artis Gilmore was sent to San Antonio for two younger players, Dave Corzine and Mark Olberding, and cash.

Gilmore had been arguably the biggest star in Chicago—literally and figuratively—in the late 1970s. But he was 32, and the Bulls liked the idea of having a local product in the paint. Corzine was from nearby Arlington Heights and had played his college ball at DePaul just down the street from the Chicago Stadium.

Corzine was durable for the Bulls, appearing in at least 80 games in all but one of his seven seasons in Chicago. But he wasn't as productive as Gilmore. Corzine's best season in Chicago was his first, when he averaged 14 points and 8.7 rebounds per game. Over 556 games with the Bulls, Corzine averaged 9.8 points and 6.3 rebounds per game.

Gilmore wasn't as good for the Spurs as he was in Chicago, but still appeared in two more NBA All-Star Games and averaged almost 17 points per game for the Spurs.

THE KEVIN LOUGHERY ERA

POP QUIZ: WHO was Michael Jordan's first head coach in the NBA? It's okay if you didn't remember Kevin Loughery's brief tenure in Chicago. It wasn't an overwhelmingly successful run.

Loughery had 11 years of head coaching experience on his resume between the NBA and ABA, including leading the New York Nets to ABA championships in 1974 and 1976. So when he arrived in Chicago in July of 1983, it felt like it might be a good hire. After all, he had led the Atlanta Hawks to the playoffs the prior season.

Chicago won only 27 games in his first season on the bench, which was good enough to land the third pick in the 1984 NBA Draft: Michael Jordan. MJ's rookie season would be Loughery's final season in Chicago. The Bulls won 38 games and qualified for the playoffs but were eliminated in the first round.

When he was fired after the 1984–85 season, only Dick Motta and Jerry Sloan had coached more games for the Bulls in the franchise's history.

Kevin Loughery spent two seasons calling the shots in Chicago.

Jordan signs his rookie contract with the Bulls.

THE DRAFT THAT CHANGED EVERYTHING

THE 1984 NBA Draft changed the history of the NBA. It was a strong, deep draft. And the future of the game was altered by the previous year's draft and a group of college players who became known as Phi Slama Jama.

Between 1982 and 1984, the players at the University of Houston were a high-flying, dominant group. In 1983, their shooting guard, Clyde Drexler, entered the NBA draft. He was selected by the Portland Trail Blazers at No. 14 overall and showed flashes of what would become a Hall of Fame career as a rookie.

Portland wasn't a good team in Drexler's rookie season, however. They wound up with the second overall pick in 1984, behind the Houston Rockets. And one of Drexler's college teammates was the top player in that year's draft.

The Rockets predictably stayed local with the top pick, selecting center Hakeem Olajuwon first. He, like Drexler, would go on to a Hall of Fame career. And the two would later be reunited in Houston with the Rockets, where they would partner to win two NBA championships.

The Blazers were on the clock with the second pick; the Bulls were patiently waiting at No. 3. With Olajuwon off the board and Drexler already in the fold, Portland opted to take Kentucky center Sam Bowie. He had been plagued by injuries during his college career and came with as many questions as he did reasons for excitement.

When the Bulls were on the clock, the name came quickly: Michael Jeffrey Jordan, guard, North Carolina.

Jordan was followed in the draft by his college teammate, Sam Perkins, who went to Dallas. Charles Barkley went to Philadelphia. John Stockton of Gonzaga was selected by the Utah Jazz at No. 16 overall.

By 1992, injuries had limited Bowie's playing time and he was in his third season in New Jersey. Drexler led the Blazers to the top of the Western Conference. But Portland had to watch the player they passed on in 1984, Jordan, beat them for his second of six NBA championships.

CARL LEWIS?

TODAY, THE NBA draft has been cut back to just two rounds. But back in 1984, the draft was 10 rounds. That year's draft was loaded with future stars; eight of the 24 players selected in the first round alone appeared in more than 1,000 regular-season games in the NBA.

When the 1984 NBA Draft took place, Michael Jordan was not the most famous individual selected by the Chicago Bulls. In fact, the Bulls picked arguably the most famous athlete in the world at the time. But most Bulls fans don't remember the selection.

With the second pick of the tenth round of the 1984 NBA Draft, No. 208 overall, the Chicago Bulls selected Carl Lewis from the University of Houston.

Yes, *that* Carl Lewis. The international track and field star who dominated the 1984 Summer Olympics in Los Angeles. The fastest man on the planet at the time.

At the 1984 Olympics, Lewis won gold in the 100 and 200 meters, was a member of the USA's gold medal–winning 4 × 100 meters relay, and won gold in the long jump as well. In his Olympic career, Lewis won nine gold medals and was one of the most accomplished athletes in the history of the Games.

He did not, however, ever appear in an NBA game—even though he was drafted by the Chicago Bulls.

Carl Lewis: Chicago Bull?

8:22
GUEST
Chicago
23
Chicago

1985

MJ'S FIRST AWARD

AFTER HE WAS drafted third overall, there was bona fide excitement around the Bulls with Michael Jordan in the lineup to start the 1984–85 season. And Jordan did little to calm that hype during a stellar first professional year.

Jordan led the entire NBA with 2,313 points scored and finished third behind Bernard King and Larry Bird in scoring average, posting a 28.2 mark as a rookie. Jordan also finished fourth in the league with 196 steals and a 2.4 steals per game.

While Bird was named the league's Most Valuable Player, Jordan was Rookie of the Year. He averaged 6.5 rebounds and 5.9 assists per game and shot 84.5 percent from the free throw line in all 82 regular-season games. He also represented the Bulls in the NBA All-Star Game that year, the first of 12 appearances in the showcase for the Bulls.

It was only the beginning of the legend, but it was an impressive first chapter.

Jordan did it all for the Bulls as a rookie.

JUNE 18
1985

ADDING OAKLEY

DURING THE 1985 NBA Draft, the Cleveland Cavaliers selected a powerful forward from Virginia Union University with the ninth overall selection. They then traded him with Calvin Duncan to the Chicago Bulls for Keith Lee and Ennis Whatley.

Over the next three years, Charles Oakley would establish himself as a menace on the glass.

Oakley averaged a double-double in his second and third seasons in the NBA.

In his sophomore campaign, Oakley's 1,074 total rebounds led the NBA and he finished second behind Charles Barkley in rebounds per game. He also led the league with 775 defensive rebounds.

Oakley followed that performance with a similar stat line in his third NBA season. He once again led the NBA in total rebounds (1,066) and defensive rebounds (740) and finished tied with Michael Cage for the NBA lead in rebounds per game, averaging 13.0.

In 241 games in three seasons in Chicago, Oakley averaged 12.2 points and 11.6 rebounds while playing 31.4 minutes per game. More importantly, he was tasked with helping protect Michael Jordan when the fouls started getting harder and the elbows were employed more frequently against a player emerging as one of the best in the game.

A young Charles Oakley with teammates Michael Jordan and Rory Sparrow

Hall of Famer Jerry Reinsdorf

JERRY BUYS THE BULLS

IN 1981, A group including tax attorney and real-estate mogul Jerry Reinsdorf bought the Chicago White Sox for $19 million. The following year, Reinsdorf sold his stake in Balcor, a company that invested in construction, to American Express for $102 million.

Already immersed in the Chicago sports ownership scene, Reinsdorf had his eyes on owning a second team. And, in 1985, another one became available.

Blackhawks owner Arthur Wirtz was growing tired of owning both tenants of Chicago Stadium. Hockey was his first love, so he remained committed to the Chicago Blackhawks. But the Bulls were another story.

So, when Reinsdorf presented him with a package of $9.2 million in 1985, a deal was done. Reinsdorf would take over controlling interest of the NBA franchise in Chicago just one year after they had drafted Michael Jordan.

Reinsdorf was elected to the Naismith Memorial Basketball Hall of Fame in 2016 with six championship trophies on display at the United Center.

KRAUSE COMES ON BOARD

WHEN JERRY REINSDORF bought the Bulls in 1985, one of the first moves he made in reshaping the basketball organization was hiring one of his scouts with the White Sox as his general manager for the Bulls. Jerry Krause, who had been a scout in both the NBA and MLB for nearly two decades, was brought in to turn around Chicago's NBA franchise.

Krause had a good eye for talent no matter the sport. He had been instrumental in his teams' drafting players like Earl "The Pearl" Monroe and Phil Jackson into the NBA. He also understood systems on the court and looked to change the way the Bulls played the game as well.

His first hire as the Bulls' general manager was Tex Winter, who came in to implement his famous triangle offense. Krause would go on to build the foundation of the Bulls' six championships around Michael Jordan; he traded for the rights to Scottie Pippen, selected Horace Grant, and traded for or signed other pieces around his core.

The players didn't necessarily get along with Krause. Jordan was close with Charles Oakley and did not agree with trading him to the Knicks for Bill Cartwright. He also didn't agree with some of the decisions Krause made in the draft.

Krause talked up a young European player named Toni Kukoč who he thought would revolutionize the team in the early 1990s, before Kukoč could come over to play for the team. Krause's hype of Kukoč made the young forward's life miserable at the 1992 Olympics when his Croatian team played the Dream Team; Jordan and Pippen made it their mission to shut him down.

Krause was named the NBA Executive of the Year twice (1988, 1996) and was inducted into the Naismith Memorial Basketball Hall of Fame for his work as an executive.

Jerry Krause was the architect of a dynasty.

TEX

Winter brought the triangle offense to Chicago.

THE FIRST THING Jerry Krause did when he assumed the role of general manager of the Chicago Bulls was call Tex Winter. Literally—he called Winter the night he got the job.

At 63, Winter was already retired. His coaching resume was already impressive. He had been head coach at Marquette, Kansas State, Washington, Northwestern, and Long Beach State in the college ranks and with the Houston Rockets for two years in the early 1970s. His teams were 120 games over .500 in college, his tactics were widely considered brilliant, and he had led four teams to the Final Four.

Winter wasn't totally out of the game in 1985. LSU had brought him in as a consultant of sorts in 1983. But when Krause called, he felt the itch to get back on the bench.

From 1985 until 1999, Winter was on the Bulls' bench. While some fans might believe his "triangle offense" was born in Chicago, he had literally written the book on it—titled *The Triple-Post Offense*—23 years before he was hired by the Bulls.

Winter survived coaching changes and roster evolutions with the Bulls, but his role in the Bulls' six championships was unquestioned. His relationship with Phil Jackson was good enough that Jackson brought him to Los Angles to help him coach the Lakers in 1999—when Winter was 77 years old.

In 2011, seven years after he officially, fully retired from the coaching profession, an 89-year-old Tex Winter was inducted into the Naismith Memorial Basketball Hall of Fame with nine NBA championship rings of his own.

The shoes that started it all for Nike—and Michael Jordan

IT'S GOTTA BE THE SHOES

THE STORY HAS now become more legendary because of the movie "Air," but the shoes have had the eyes of millions of basketball fans for four decades.

Coming into the NBA as the third overall pick out of North Carolina, Michael Jordan was being courted by all of the big shoe companies at the time. Converse and Adidas made a strong play for Jordan, but Nike blew him and his family away with their pitch. On October 26, 1984, Jordan signed the richest deal in NBA history: five years, $2.5 million.

In April of 1985, Nike released the first line of Air Jordan sneakers. At the time, the NBA's policy stated shoes worn in games must be at least 51 percent white for uniformity. Breaking that rule would result in a $5,000 fine per game. Nike agreed to pay the fines for every game that Jordan wore his signature shoe, which featured more red and black—Bulls colors—than white. Nike even used the banning of the shoes as a marketing campaign.

Nike's goal was to sell $3 million of shoes in the first three years after launch. They sold $126 million in the first year. The rest is shoe, basketball, and pop culture history.

In 1997, Nike introduced the Jordan brand using the "Jumpman" logo created for the launch of his signature shoe. The Jumpman logo originated from a photo of Jordan by Jacobus Rentmeester for *Life* magazine before the 1984 Summer Olympics.

OCTOBER 29

1985

PAX

ON OCTOBER 29, 1985, the Bulls signed a young guard who had played his college ball at nearby Notre Dame. After two seasons in San Antonio, the former first-round pick hit the market and he signed in Chicago.

John Paxson would spend the next 35 years with the Bulls.

For nine seasons, Paxson would play an important role on the floor for the Bulls. He hit one of the most memorable shots in franchise history. In Game 6 of the 1993 NBA Finals, Horace Grant kicked the ball to Paxson, who knocked down a three-pointer with 3.9 seconds left to secure the Bulls' third consecutive championship. Paxson was a member of the Bulls' first three title-winning teams.

When he retired from playing in 1994, Paxson served as an assistant coach on Phil Jackson's staff. He was part of the group that helped lead the Bulls to their historic 72-win season and subsequent championship. Pax then moved to the broadcast booth, where he spent seven years calling Bulls games.

In April 2003, when Jerry Krause retired, Paxson was named the team's general manager. Six years later he was elevated to the top job in basketball operations, bringing in Gar Forman as the general manager. After a long front office tenure that saw its share of ups and downs, Paxson stepped aside in 2020.

"When I came here in 1985, I never imagined what the Chicago Bulls would mean to me more than 35 years later," Paxson said in a statement released in 2020 when he stepped back from his role as the Bulls' top basketball executive. "I've had the rare opportunity to see this team as a player, broadcaster, and executive, and at every turn I've been fortunate to experience what makes this organization so special."

John Paxson spent decades with the Bulls as a player and executive.

Stereo
Tape
38 SPORTS
CELTICS
33
BULLS
CELTICS
00
BULLS
40
BULLS
20
CELTICS
BASF
Audio
Tapes

APRIL 20

1986

63 POINTS? IN A PLAYOFF GAME?

AFTER MICHAEL JORDAN won the NBA's Rookie of the Year Award, there were high hopes that his sophomore season would lead to bigger and better things. Unfortunately, a broken foot cost him 64 games during the regular season.

Jordan still averaged 22.7 points and 2.1 steals per game in 18 regular-season appearances and represented the Bulls in the NBA All-Star Game for a second time in as many seasons. But how much he could bring to the court at the end of the year was a very real question.

Thankfully, the good news was that the Bulls surrounding him were good enough to get into the playoffs despite his season being limited. The bad news: the Boston Celtics—with five future Hall of Famers—were waiting for them in the first round of the postseason.

In Game 1 of the series, Jordan scored 49 of the Bulls' 104 points on 18 of 36 shooting in 43 minutes. He also collected four rebounds and was credited with two assists, two steals and one blocked shot in a 19-point loss. That set the table for arguably the greatest performance in a postseason loss in NBA history. On April 20, 1986, in Game 2 of the series, Jordan started to show the world that he was going to transition from star to legend.

Jordan broke Elgin Baylor's postseason record, scoring 63 points in a performance that led Larry Bird to say "That was God disguised as Michael Jordan."

Matched up primarily against Hall of Famer Dennis Johnson and All-Star Danny Ainge, Jordan had a hand in his face the entire night. He made 22 of 41 shots from the field and 19 of 21 free throws in the game. Many people forget that he also had five rebounds, six assists, three steals, and two blocks that night.

The Celtics won the game 135–131 in double overtime. But that night, Jordan put the NBA on notice of what was to come.

According to Basketball Reference, Jordan's 63-point night produced a Game Score of 47.2, which still ranks eighth in NBA postseason history. That stat has been calculated since the 1984 playoffs. One of the seven performances that ranks higher: Jordan's 56-point performance in the series-clinching win against the Miami Heat on April 29, 1992.

The Celtics finished the sweep in the only game played in Chicago, and Jordan didn't score nearly as well as he had in the first two games. Boston held Jordan to 19 points on 8 of 18 shooting in the series-ending game; Jordan fouled out after playing 39 minutes. But he came one assist away from a triple-double in the final game of the Bulls' postseason; he had 10 rebounds and 9 assists in the 122–104 loss.

In four decades since Jordan's incredible 63-point effort, no player had matched his performance that night in Boston. There have been 51 playoff games in NBA history in which a player scored at least 50 points. Eight were authored by Jordan, who also scored 56 in 1992 and 55 on three occasions in the postseason.

"God disguised as Michael Jordan" avoids the defense of Larry Legend.

MAY 19

1986

DOUG COLLINS

ON MAY 19, 1986, the Chicago Bulls introduced a new head coach they hoped would elevate the team's play around superstar Michael Jordan.

Doug Collins had played well enough at Illinois State to be the first overall pick in the 1973 NBA draft by the Philadelphia 76ers. He played eight seasons for Philadelphia and was an NBA All-Star four times. Injuries cut his playing career short, but he quickly turned his competitive spirit to coaching.

With his curly hair and demonstrative coaching style, Collins became a popular coach in Chicago. The improving play of the Bulls under his leadership also helped. The team's record improved by 10 wins in each of his first two seasons as head coach, and the team made the playoffs in both years. The Bulls were 50–32 in Collins' second season as head coach and advanced to the second round of the playoffs but lost to the Detroit Pistons in five games.

In Collins' third season on the bench, the Bulls won 47 games in the regular season and advanced all the way to the Eastern Conference Finals, where they ran into the Pistons yet again. The Bulls took the Pistons to six games, but were eliminated by their hated rivals once again.

Surprisingly, Collins was fired on July 6, 1989 and replaced by one of his assistant coaches, Phil Jackson.

Collins and Jordan led the Bulls to another level on the court.

Jordan attacking the rim in Seattle

THE 1987 DUNK CONTEST

ON FEBRUARY 8, 1987, the NBA held the Slam Dunk Contest before its annual All-Star Game in Seattle. The stage was set for Michael Jordan to take another step into superstardom. Reigning champion Spud Webb was not competing, and previous champ Dominique Wilkins was injured and not part of the festivities.

The field was still a very good one. Clyde Drexler and Jerome Kersey from Portland were formidable opponents. Johnny Dawkins, Tom Chambers, Terence Stansbury, and Dominique's younger brother, Gerald Wilkins, were also in the mix. Also competing was Jordan's future teammate for three championships, Ron Harper.

Jordan dropped a two-handed cradle in his first attempt and then a 360 off a bounce for his second dunk. Okay, nice. Kersey and Stansbury—who scored a 49 for his patented Statue of Liberty—were impressive in their early dunks. Michael needed to bring it, even if the crowd was behind him.

The final of the competition was Jordan versus Kersey. Kersey did well; Jordan exploded.

Jordan performed a gorgeous reverse windmill that scored a 48, a split-legged one-handed dunk that also received a 48 from the judges, and then a baseline windmill that took the roof off the building for a 50.

For the first time, Michael Jordan was the NBA's Slam Dunk Contest champion. His performance in this contest raised the bar for the entire competition, and set the stage for an iconic contest the following year when the NBA brought the event to Jordan's building—the Chicago Stadium.

Jordan climbed to the top of the NBA's scoring ranks for the first time.

JORDAN'S FIRST SCORING TITLE

THE 1986–87 SEASON was a revelation for the NBA and an awakening for players who thought they could compete with Michael Jordan.

After missing most of the previous season because of a broken foot, Jordan returned on a mission. He appeared in all 82 games that year and attacked defenses on a nightly basis. When the regular season came to a close, Jordan had averaged 37.1 points per game—the highest mark of his career.

Jordan didn't waste time asserting his dominance, scoring 50 in a 108–103 win over the Knicks at Madison Square Garden on opening night. He followed that up with 41 at Cleveland in a 94–89 win over the Cavaliers.

In November—the first month of the season—Jordan averaged 37.5 points per game in 13 contests. He wasn't only scoring, however. Jordan also averaged 6.2 rebounds and 2.5 assists per game that month. Jordan topped 40 points in six of the 13 games and had at least eight rebounds five times.

Between November 28 and December 18, Jordan scored at least 40 points in 11 of 12 games; he was held to 11 by Milwaukee on December 13. He only failed to reach the 40-point mark four times in 15 games in December, averaging 37.4 points per game for the second calendar month of the season.

Jordan recorded his second game of at least 50 points on January 8 when he put 53 on the Portland Trail Blazers. Three games later, on January 17 against the Philadelphia 76ers, Jordan scored 47 and grabbed 10 rebounds for his second double-double of the campaign. He finished the month of January averaging 36.6 points per game in 14 appearances.

His scoring average went up to 38.4 points per game in 12 appearances in February; he was held under 30 points only once in the month. Jordan recorded his third double-double of the season against the Atlanta Hawks on February 24 when he scored 34 with 12 rebounds. The next game two days later, Jordan scored 58 in a 128–113 win over the New Jersey Nets. He also averaged 3.7 steals per game in February.

Jordan reached 61 points in Detroit on March 4, a 125–120 overtime win. He came back with 58 points and eight steals against the Sixers on March 24. He appeared in 19 games in March, a busy month. Jordan averaged 35.6 points and 3.7 steals per game. Jordan also added 5.1 rebounds and 5.6 assists per game in a balanced month that filled the box score almost every night.

The Bulls were chasing a playoff berth once again, and were able to clinch a spot before the end of the regular season in large part because Jordan continued to score whenever he wanted. Knowing the Bulls would face the Boston Celtics in the first round of the 1987 playoffs, Jordan only played 25 minutes in the season finale; he scored just 17 points but also had eight assists in the last game of the regular season.

But in the two games before sitting against Boston, Jordan put the finishing touches on a historic scoring season. He had 50 and nine rebounds in Milwaukee on April 13 and then matched his season-high with 61 (and 10 rebounds) against the Atlanta Hawks in the final home game of the regular season. Jordan had two double-doubles in April; he also had 10 assists with 34 points on April 10 in Philadelphia.

More impressively, Jordan scored a total of 3,041 points. The only other player to that point who had reached 3,000 points in an NBA regular season was Wilt Chamberlain, who did it three times during his historic career. No player has reached the benchmark since Jordan did it nearly 40 years ago.

Jordan claimed the first of his 10 league scoring titles that season while averaging an astounding 40 minutes per night. He also averaged 5.2 rebounds, 4.6 assists, 2.9 steals, and 1.5 blocks per game that season, the most impressive regular season of his young career.

PIPPEN ON BOARD

WHEN THE 1987 NBA Draft began, all of the talk was about the presumed No. 1 overall pick. Would the San Antonio Spurs select David Robinson even though his required military service as a graduate of the Naval Academy would keep him out of the league for some time?

The Spurs did select Robinson first. But it was a trade in the middle of the top ten overall selections that changed the trajectory of the NBA for the next decade.

The Seattle SuperSonics owned the No. 5 pick, and the Bulls owned Nos. 8 and 10 in the first round. Seattle selected a skinny forward from Central Arkansas named Scottie Pippen; at No. 8, the Bulls selected forward Olden Polynice from Virginia.

Seattle and Chicago worked out a trade that would swap Pippen and Polynice; the deal also included a swap of 1989 first-round picks, and the Bulls also sent a second-round pick in 1988 to the Sonics.

The first-round pick the Bulls received in 1989 was used on point guard B. J. Armstrong out of Iowa.

Polynice would not average better than 8.3 points per game in three and a half seasons with the Sonics before he was traded to the Clippers during the 1990–91 season. Pippen would go on to become one of the best all-around small forwards in the history of the game.

Pippen was the perfect complement to Air Jordan.

Grant was the Bulls' other pick in the top ten in 1987.

HORACE

WITH THE 10TH overall selection in the 1987 NBA Draft, the Chicago Bulls selected a power forward from Clemson named Horace Grant.

Grant and his goggles came to Chicago, where the Bulls already had one of the better young power forwards in the NBA, Charles Oakley. Grant had been a second-team All-American at Clemson and had similar size to Oakley, helping the Bulls bulk up their interior.

In the seven seasons that would follow, Grant would emerge as one of the better players in the game. Always in the shadow of Jordan and Pippen, Grant wasn't named an NBA All-Star until the 1993–94 season—while Jordan was playing baseball. But he was a critical piece of the Bulls' first three championship teams.

Grant really emerged as a bona fide NBA star during the 1990 Eastern Conference Finals against the Pistons. He averaged a double-double in that series, even though the Bulls lost in seven games.

Over 546 regular-season games with the Bulls, Grant averaged 12.6 points and 8.6 rebounds per game. He averaged a double-double twice for the Bulls (1991–92 and 1993–94). With Jordan still retired, he opted to sign with the Orlando Magic as a free agent during the summer of 1994.

FEBRUARY 6

1988

THE LEGENDARY '88 DUNK CONTEST

THE 1988 NBA All-Star Game was in Chicago, which meant the Slam Dunk Contest was at the Chicago Stadium. And Michael Jordan was the defending champion.

But his work was cut out for him. Previous champions Dominique Wilkins and Spud Webb were both in the event this time; neither of them had performed the previous year. Portland's Clyde Drexler was also back for another attempt.

The full list of participants in the 1988 Slam Dunk Contest saw Cadillac Anderson of the San Antonio Spurs, Jerome Kersey of the Portland Trail Blazers and Otis Smith of the Golden State Warriors join Drexler, Webb, Wilkins and Jordan.

The basketball world was excited for a rematch of Wilkins versus Jordan. In 1985, Wilkins beat Jordan in the contest for his first title. As the contest progressed it became clear hoops fans were going to get what they wanted in the final.

The "Human Highlight Film" was at his best, as was Jordan. In front of a full house of more than 18,000 fans, Wilkins and Jordan combined for a perfect score of 50 on four of their final six dunks.

On Wilkins's final attempt, he attacked the rim with a ferocious two-hand windmill jam that brought the crowd to its feet. The dunk was only scored a 45, however. Which meant Jordan needed at least a 49 on his final attempt.

Jordan backed up to the far end of the court and the anticipation was at a peak. He took off from the free throw line, double clutched in the air, and slammed it home. The judges gave Jordan a perfect score of 50—and the championship.

Among the judges for this historic Slam Dunk Contest were Chicago Bears Hall of Fame running back Gale Sayers and former NBA player and then-Los Angeles Dodgers Vice President Tom Hawkins, who had gone to Parker High School in Chicago before playing at Notre Dame. They were joined on the panel by NBA Hall of Famer Gail Goodrich and former NBA players Johnny Green and Randy Smith.

Because the judges had a unique Chicago influence for an event that took place at Chicago Stadium, there was some controversy surrounding how Wilkins's dunks were scored. In a February 2013 issue of *Sports Illustrated*, Kersey told Lee Jenkins:

"He was so high off the ground, with such power and grace, that all the players on the bench were saying, 'Fifty.' His first two dunks of the finals were 50s. But for some reason they gave him 45 on the last one. It was like, Are you kidding? How can that be? We just looked at one another on the bench and ducked our heads. The expression on Nique's face was, 'What do I have to do here?'"

Some felt Wilkins ccould or should have won. But everyone acknowledged that it was Jordan's day on his home floor in arguably the greatest dunk contest ever.

You can still find numerous videos of this amazing Slam Dunk Contest on YouTube. The NBA posted a highlight reel from the contest in 2017, and it has nearly 1 million views.

One of the defining images of Jordan at the Chicago Stadium

HOSTING THE 1988 ALL-STAR GAME

IN 1988, THE Chicago Bulls and Michael Jordan were emerging as the most exciting team to watch in the league. And the NBA's annual All-Star Game was played at the Chicago Stadium, Michael's house.

The game's rosters were loaded with incredible names, but Jordan received the most votes from the fans that year (more than 1.1 million). He was joined in the starting lineup for the Eastern Conference by Larry Bird, Dominique Wilkins, Moses Malone, and Isiah Thomas. The Western Conference's starting five was Magic Johnson, Karl Malone, Hakeem Olajuwon, Alex English, and Fat Lever.

Nine of the ten starters in the game would eventually be inducted into the Naismith Memorial Basketball Hall of Fame. The benches were also loaded with future Hall of Famers: Charles Barkley, Patrick Ewing, Kevin McHale, Maurice Cheeks, Clyde Drexler, Kareem Abdul-Jabbar, and James Worthy.

It was an absolute spectacle. And the night belonged to Jordan.

The East won the game 138–133, and Jordan led the game with 40 points. He was named the All-Star Game MVP on his home floor.

Of course MJ was the MVP of the Chicago All-Star Game.

MAY 7

1989

Poor Craig Ehlo

THE SHOT

ON MAY 7, 1989, the Chicago Bulls entered a game at Coliseum at Richfield in Ohio against a Cleveland Cavaliers team that had them tied in a best-of-five series. The win-or-go-home scenario made for a dramatic game for both franchises. It was close. And it ended with an exclamation point.

Chicago entered the fourth quarter down six. They clawed their way back to within one in the closing seconds. Everyone on the planet knew who was going to take the shot.

That Cavs team had a tough defensive group in the back court. Mark Price, Ron Harper, and Craig Ehlo did a decent job against Jordan most nights. On this night, Jordan was out to move his team on to the second round of the Eastern Conference playoffs—and he wouldn't be denied.

As the clock wound down, Jordan left the floor with Ehlo in his face. He elevated . . . and stayed in the air long enough for Ehlo to fly by. Jordan released "The Shot" just before the clock expired. It found the bottom of the net, and the Bulls escaped with a 101–100 victory.

That shot, and the fist pumps from Jordan that followed, became one of the iconic images of his career. Jordan finished with a game-high 44 points that night and also contributed nine rebounds and a Bulls-leading six assists.

Ehlo led the Cavs with 24 points that night and could have been a hero in Ohio. Unfortunately, the image of Jordan in the air became the most memorable moment of his career.

Jordan's acrobatic attacks of the rim made the dunk contest special.

JUNE
1988

JORDAN DOMINATES AWARD SEASON

IF THE 1986–87 regular season was impressive, Michael Jordan took his game to another entire level the following season. With some significant additions to the roster—notably including Scottie Pippen and Horace Grant—Jordan emerged as the unquestioned best player in the game.

With his Slam Dunk Contest victory and All-Star Game MVP on his home court as two key moments during the regular season, Jordan's complete season was unlike any we had ever seen in the NBA.

Jordan won the league scoring title, averaging 35 points per game. He also led the league in steals, averaging 3.2 per game. He added 1.6 blocked shots per night as well that year.

Those efforts were good enough for Jordan to win the NBA's Defensive Player of the Year (DPOY) award. At 24, Jordan was the second-youngest player to win the award to that point; the league started distributing the DPOY in 1983, and only Alvin Robertson (23) had won it at a younger age.

Jordan was also named the NBA's Most Valuable Player for his remarkable season. At that time, the only players to win the league's MVP award before their 24th birthdays were Moses Malone, Kareem Abdul-Jabbar, Wes Unseld, Wilt Chamberlain, and Bill Russell.

No player had ever won the NBA's MVP and DPOY Awards in the same season, however. And in the nearly four decades since, only Hakeem Olajuwon (1994) and Giannis Antetokounmpo (2020) have won the awards in the same season.

The only other players to win an MVP and a DPOY in their careers are David Robinson and Kevin Garnett. Jordan is the only guard to ever win both prestigious awards in his NBA career.

Jordan collecting one of his awards during a historic season

JUNE 27
1989

DRAFTING A KING AND B. J.

WHEN THE BULLS lost Orlando Woolridge to free agency in 1986, the New Jersey Nets compensated the Bulls by sending three draft picks to Chicago. The Bulls received the Nets' second-round picks in 1988 and 1989 and New Jersey's first-round pick in 1989.

At the conclusion of the 1988–89 season, that first rounder from the Nets landed sixth overall in a draft that had some interesting prospects. The Bulls also owned the 18th overall selection, giving a team that was on the rise the opportunity to add two potential contributors to their roster.

Oddly enough, the Bulls had actually traded that 18th overall selection to Seattle in the deal that landed Scottie Pippen in 1987. But two years later, the Sonics sent it back to Chicago for Brad Sellers.

After watching Pervis Ellison, Danny Ferry, Sean Elliott, Glen Rice, and J. R. Reid come off the board, the Bulls were on the clock. A couple local products, Nick Anderson and Tim Hardaway, were available. But the Bulls opted to select the *Sporting News* College Player of the Year out of Oklahoma, center Stacey King.

With guard help still in mind, the Bulls watched as both Anderson and Hardaway—and Mookie Blaylock, Dana Barros, and power forward Shawn Kemp—were taken before they were back on the clock at No. 18. But a point guard from Iowa was still available; the Bulls selected B. J. Armstrong.

Both King and Armstrong were contributors to the Bulls' first three championships, and Armstrong appeared in the 1994 NBA All-Star Game representing the Bulls as well before he was selected by the Toronto Raptors in the expansion draft in 1995.

Armstrong became a key contributor for the Bulls.

JUNE 27

1988

Cartwright was just right for the Bulls' roster.

OAKLEY FOR CARTWRIGHT

ON JUNE 27, 1988, the Bulls made one of the more infamous trades in team history. Charles Oakley had established himself as a physical enforcer and one of the best rebounders in the NBA over the first three years of his career. But the Bulls were looking for more of a traditional low-post threat and found a partner to make a blockbuster trade.

Chicago traded Oakley with a first-round draft pick (Rod Strickland) and a third-round draft pick (Phil Stinnie) in the 1988 NBA Draft to the New York Knicks for veteran center Bill Cartwright, a first-round draft pick (Will Perdue) and third-round draft pick (Derrick Lewis) in the 1988 NBA Draft.

At the time of the trade, Cartwright was a few weeks away from his 31st birthday. He had averaged 16.8 points and 7.1 rebounds per game over eight seasons with the Knicks, but missed the entire 1984–85 season because of a foot injury.

Al Bianchi, the Knicks' general manager at the time, told the media: "We have really solidified the power-forward position. I think we can walk away saying that the Knicks are happy and the Chicago Bulls filled their need for a center."

Why did Chicago make the trade? Jerry Krause told the media "The development of Horace Grant helped us make such a deal. We feel Horace can be a quality player and develop like Charles Oakley.'' He was right.

As Chicago built their triangle offense, Cartwright arrived with a toughness in the post that complimented the roster being built around Jordan. The additions of Cartwright and Perdue in the paint proved pivotal in the Bulls winning their first three championships.

Oakley would return to Chicago much later in his career, but this trade—which was questioned at the time—ended up working brilliantly for the team.

JULY 10
1989

PHIL'S IN CHARGE

PHIL JACKSON HAD a nice career as an NBA player. He won an NBA championship with the Knicks in 1973 and appeared in 807 regular-season games over 12 seasons with the Knicks and Nets.

He began his coaching career as an assistant in New Jersey at only 33 years of age. After three seasons with the Nets and six years away from NBA coaching, he took a job as an assistant in Chicago. When Doug Collins was relieved of his duties in a surprising move, the choice for his replacement was clear.

On July 10, 1989, the Bulls promoted Jackson to the head coaching position.

The Bulls won 55 games in Jackson's first season as the head coach and advanced to the Eastern Conference Finals, where they lost—again—to the Detroit Pistons. Chicago won 10 games in that first postseason under Jackson's leadership.

The 1990–91 season was just different. The Bulls won 61 games in the regular season and finished first in the Central Division. In the postseason they were as dominant as any team in NBA history. The Bulls swept the Knicks in the best-of-five first round and eliminated the 76ers in five games to set up a rematch with Detroit in the conference finals. This time around, the Bulls swept the Pistons.

Chicago then beat the Lakers in five games to claim their first NBA championship.

In the seven seasons that followed, the Bulls never missed the playoffs. Chicago would win five more championships with Jackson calling the shots, becoming a dynasty.

Over his nine seasons as the head coach of the Bulls, Chicago posted a 545–193 record in the regular season and 111–41 record in the playoffs.

Jackson became the greatest coach in Bulls history.

Hodges with a star-studded lineup for the three-point contest in 1991

THREE-POINT CONTEST DOMINANCE

IN 1990, THE entire NBA took its collective talents to South Beach as the Miami Heat hosted the NBA All-Star Game. For the fifth time, skills events were included in the weekend's festivities, and the three-point contest was loaded with stars.

Boston's Larry Bird had won each of the first three contests from 1986 to 1989 before Dale Ellis won it in 1989; Bird did not compete that year. But he returned in 1990 to face off against a field that included Michael Jordan, Reggie Miller, Mark Price, Craig Hodges, Craig Ehlo, Bob Hansen, and Jon Sundvold.

Bird would not win the title that year. Instead, the title went to Hodges—and he held onto the crown for three consecutive years.

Among the other future Hall of Famers Hodges would beat in the three-point contest in the following two years were Clyde Drexler and Tim Hardaway in 1991 and Dražen Petrović, Mitch Richmond, and John Stockton in 1992. Also in the 1992 contest: the father of the player who would revolutionize three-point shooting, Dell Curry.

Mark Price would take the crown away in 1993, the first of two consecutive wins for him. To this day, only Bird and Hodges have won three titles in the event.

FEBRUARY 14

1990

MJ IN NO. 12?

MICHAEL JORDAN WAS an established superstar well before the 1989–90 season. And Jordan memorabilia was already the hottest on the market. It was so popular that some people went to extreme measures to get their hands on unique Jordan pieces.

Which is why, on Valentine's Day in 1990, seeing Jordan take the floor in a red Bulls jersey without his name on the back—or his trademark No. 23—was incredibly strange.

Before the game, someone had broken into the Bulls' locker room in Orlando and stolen his jersey. The Bulls didn't have time to come up with another jersey for him to wear, and had only packed one for the trip. So Jordan put on an unnamed No. 12 jersey.

The Magic found out quickly that Michael wasn't someone they wanted to play against when he wasn't happy.

Jordan played 47 minutes in the wrong number, scoring 49 points on 21 of 43 shooting. He also collected seven rebounds in the game. Orlando won the game 135–129, but the image of Jordan wearing the wrong number became infamous.

A stolen jersey created an infamous number swap for MJ.

MARCH 28
1990

A NICE NIGHT IN CLEVELAND

ON MARCH 28, 1990, the Bulls traveled to Cleveland to face a Cavs team against whom they had some memorable battles. For Michael Jordan, this night would prove to be one of the most memorable regular season games of his legendary career.

The players surrounding Jordan in the Bulls' lineup didn't have a great night. The rest of the team made only 19 of 50 field goal attempts in the game, and only Horace Grant finished with more than nine points; Scottie Pippen was held to seven points on three of ten shooting.

Jordan had to win the game almost on his own. And he did just that.

He did almost everything that night. Jordan pulled down 18 rebounds; no other Bull had more than eight. He had six assists; only Pippen (seven) had more. He added four steals; Pippen had five.

But it was the offense that made this night special for Michael. Jordan made 23 of 37 shots from the field and 21 of 23 from the charity stripe. When the final horn sounded, Jordan had posted a career-high 69 points in a 117–113 victory.

Jordan loved putting up big numbers against the Cavs.

1990

The Bulls-Pistons rivalry was as physical as it gets.

THE BAD BOYS

CHICAGO AND DETROIT have long been rivals in sports. Whether it's the Bears and Lions, White Sox and Tigers, Blackhawks and Red Wings, or Bulls and Pistons, fans in the two cities do not get along. And the players in each sport rarely consider each other friends, either.

As the Bulls were rising in the late 1980s, they ran into the big, tough Pistons in the playoffs too often for comfort. The "Bad Boys" had targeted Michael Jordan and Scottie Pippen with physical play during their games, and that led to Detroit wins more times than not.

Even with Jordan having his historic 1987–88 regular season, the Pistons knocked the Bulls out of the playoffs in five games in the Eastern Conference Semifinals. In 1989, the Bulls made it to the Eastern Conference Finals, where Detroit was waiting yet again. And the Pistons beat the Bulls in six games that time.

The Bulls thought they had the right roster to unseat the defending NBA champions in 1990 when they met for the second straight year in the Eastern Conference Finals. The series would go a full seven games, but Detroit prevailed on their way to back-to-back NBA titles.

In his career, Michael Jordan averaged 29.7 points in 64 regular-season games against the Pistons. He attempted 601 free throws against Detroit—the second-most of any team he faced (he attempted 651 against Milwaukee).

To say the Jordan-era Bulls hated the Pistons might be an understatement, and after three straight postseason losses they knew who they had to beat to get to the mountain top.

BE LIKE MIKE

IF YOU'RE AN NBA fan of a certain age, there's a hook to a song from a popular commercial that automatically makes you want to sing along. When the lyrics begin, it's impossible to not join in.

"Sometimes I dream, that he is me."

In 1991, with the Bulls on their way to their first NBA championship and before the Summer Olympics in which Michael Jordan would take the entire world over and emerge as a global superstar, Gatorade dropped one of the most iconic television commercials ever made.

"Be Like Mike" showed kids playing basketball with their tongues wagging, Michael on a playground with young players, and all of them consuming the refreshing sports drink.

Ira Antelis composed the song, but not without some controversy. Gatorade originally wanted to use the song "I Wanna Be Like You" from the Disney movie *The Jungle Book* in the commercial, but negotiations between the two companies to use the song never worked out. Antelis has claimed in the years since that he put together the iconic song in 15 minutes, and the rest is marketing history.

So, let's all sing along:

Sometimes I dream
That he is me
You've got to see that's how I dream to be
I dream I move, I dream I groove
Like Mike
If I could Be Like Mike
Like Mike
Oh, if I could Be Like Mike
Be Like Mike, Be Like Mike
Again I try
Just need to fly
For just one day if I could
Be that way
I dream I move
I dream I groove
Like Mike
If I could Be Like Mike
I wanna be, I wanna be
Like Mike
Oh, if I could Be Like Mike
Sometimes I feel
This dream is real
The shots I make nobody else would take
I seem to soar
Can hear the roar
Like Mike
If I could be like Mike

A commercial song tied Jordan and Gatorade forever.

DIVISION CHAMPS

AFTER GETTING BOUNCED from the playoffs for the third straight year by the Pistons in 1990, the Bulls were out to prove they were the best team in the NBA from the opening jump of the 1990–91 season.

Of course, the Bulls started the season with three straight losses, including a 124-116 opening night loss on their home floor to the Philadelphia 76ers.

But the Bulls would get things right in Minnesota for their first win of the season, and they would start rolling. With a 98–86 win over the Pistons on Christmas Day, the Bulls were 18–9 and starting to look like the top team in the Eastern Conference.

Between February 4 and March 1 the Bulls won 11 straight games, including wins in Detroit, against the Knicks at Madison Square Garden, and over the Celtics in Chicago. The final win of that streak, the Bulls' fourth winning streak of at least five games, made Chicago's record 41–14.

Chicago finished the regular season with a 108–100 win over the Pistons at Chicago Stadium to give the Bulls 61 regular-season wins, the most in franchise history to that point. And, for the first time since the league expanded and realigned, the Bulls were division champions.

Jordan and the Bulls finally claimed a division title.

1991

Another MVP for MJ

1991 MVP

MICHAEL JORDAN DID his part in helping lead the Bulls to the best record in franchise history and first Central Division title during the 1990–91 season. He appeared in all 82 regular-season games and led the league in scoring, averaging 31.5 points per game.

Jordan added 6 rebounds and 5.5 assists with 2.7 steals and 1 blocked shot per game to an impressive resume. For the fourth consecutive season, Jordan was named to the NBA's All-Defensive First Team at the end of the season and was also named to the All-NBA First Team as well.

And, for the second time in his career, Jordan was named the NBA's Most Valuable Player.

Excluding the 1985–86 season, in which Jordan dealt with a broken foot, Jordan's scoring average was his lowest since his rookie season. The emergence of Scottie Pippen, who averaged a then-career-high 17.8 points per game that season, took some of the burden off Jordan and Chicago rolled to the best record in franchise history to that point.

Magic Johnson had won the two MVP Awards between Jordan's first in 1988 and this one, and they were on a collision course to meet for the ultimate prize.

1991

PISTONS DEFEATED—FINALLY

AFTER THE DETROIT Pistons eliminated the Bulls in three consecutive postseasons, Michael Jordan instructed his teammates that they needed to be bigger and stronger if they wanted to beat them. So they went to work to become more physically and mentally tough before the 1990–91 season.

Chicago finished the regular season with the best record in the Eastern Conference, and the postseason script played out perfectly for fans. The Bulls would get a third straight shot at the Pistons in the Conference Finals.

This time, Jordan and Co. would not be denied. Chicago won the first two games on their home court. Jordan took over in Game 2 and scored 35 points to lead the Bulls.

With Game 3 in Detroit, the Bulls knew the emotions would shift. Jordan answered the bell with 33 points, seven rebounds, seven assists, three steals, and five blocked shots. Pippen added 26 points, 10 rebounds, and four assists. And the Bulls were one win away from the first NBA Finals in franchise history.

The Bulls played a nearly perfect Game 4. Chicago took a 17-point lead to the fourth quarter, and they were clearly mentally ready for everything the Pistons tried to do to get them off their game. Jordan scored 29 points with eight rebounds and eight assists, and Pippen had another double-double, this time with 23 points and 10 assists.

In the closing seconds of the Bulls' sweep, the Pistons' starters walked off the floor without shaking hands with the Bulls. The move stunned many onlookers and fans. Jordan averaged 29.8 points, 7 rebounds, 5.3 assists, 2.3 steals, and 1.8 blocks per game in the series. More importantly, the Bulls' hard work had paid off.

The Bulls were moving on to face Magic Johnson and the Lakers in the NBA Finals—and they had finally beaten the "Bad Boys."

Beating the Pistons propelled the Bulls to greatness.

THE FIRST CHAMPIONSHIP

AFTER WINNING THE Central Division with 61 victories in the regular season and then finally knocking off the Pistons in the Eastern Conference Finals, one could easily imagine the Bulls having a bit of a letdown in the NBA Finals. They were rolling, however; Chicago won 11 of their 12 games en route to the NBA Finals, but the experienced Los Angeles Lakers were waiting for them.

The Lakers were the road team to start the series, but they had been through their share of championship series. Led by Magic Johnson, who had won back-to-back MVP awards before Michael Jordan won it in 1991, they were ready to re-establish their authority over the league.

LA won the first game of the series 93–91 at the Chicago Stadium in dramatic fashion, taking a 1–0 series lead. But from there, the Bulls' defense was just too much for even the veteran Lakers to withstand.

The Bulls held the Lakers to only 86 points in Game 2, winning by 21 points. The third game of the series required overtime, but the Bulls pulled away and won by eight. Chicago won Game 4 by 15 points, holding the Lakers to only 82 points.

In the fifth and final game of the series, the Lakers scored their highest total of the series (101), but it wasn't enough. Michael Jordan (30) and Scottie Pippen (team-high 32 points) led the Bulls to the victory. Jordan claimed his first of six NBA Finals MVP Awards, and the Chicago Bulls were NBA champions for the first time in franchise history.

A dream matchup: Michael against Magic in the Finals

APRIL
1992

Pippen developed into a star in Chicago.

RUNNING IT BACK

THE BULLS WASTED no time putting the NBA on notice that they weren't satisfied with one championship when the 1991–92 season began. They won their home opener by 20 over the 76ers before losing their next two games. They then rolled off a 14-game winning streak.

When the calendar flipped over to 1992, the Bulls had an NBA-best 24–4 record. And, after losing their first game of the new year in Milwaukee, the Bulls went on another 13-game winning streak to extend their ridiculous record to 37–5.

Chicago finished the regular season with the best record in the NBA—and the best record in franchise history. At 67–15, they were primed to make another deep playoff run.

Michael Jordan once again led the team, but Scottie Pippen and Horace Grant really came into their own after winning their first championship. Pippen averaged a career-high 21 points and added 7.7 rebounds and 7 assists per game. Grant averaged a double-double (14.2 points, 10 rebounds).

The Bulls won the Central Division for the second straight year.

JORDAN'S THIRD MVP

THE 1991–92 SEASON was about doing it again for Michael Jordan. He had conquered the basketball world, winning his first NBA championship the previous season. But the all-time greats did it more than once. And Michael wanted to be in the same conversation as Magic Johnson and Larry Bird.

He did nothing to calm the fears of the rest of the league. Jordan led the league in scoring for the sixth straight season and appeared in his eighth consecutive NBA All-Star Game. And now he had players around him who were helping carry the burden of being defending NBA champions.

Jordan was once again named NBA All-Defensive First Team and All-NBA First Team, and he won his third NBA MVP award.

At that time, the only players who had won three NBA MVP Awards were Bill Russell, Wilt Chamberlain, Kareem Abdul-Jabbar, Moses Malone, Bird, and Magic. For Bird and Magic, it certainly appeared that their careers were headed to the league's rearview mirror as Jordan became the face of the NBA.

Jordan picking up another MVP for the trophy case

THE KNICKS RIVALRY

THE BULLS AND Knicks rivalry started to grow as New York developed a more physical roster around Patrick Ewing, who had watched Michael Jordan knock down a game-winning shot against his Georgetown Hoyas in the 1982 NCAA championship game. In the spring of 1992, Jordan and Ewing became one of the most watched matchups in the NBA.

As the Bulls were looking to defend their first championship, the Knicks were standing in their way in the second round of the Eastern Conference playoffs. The series went the distance, with the Bulls winning the decisive seventh game by 29.

In that series, John Starks emerged as a bona fide nemesis for the Bulls. He scored 27 points in the Knicks' Game 6 win and 18 in the finale. With Ewing, Starks, Derek Harper, and Jordan's friend, Charles Oakley, the Knicks became one of the Bulls' toughest tests during their championship dynasty. During Chicago's six championship seasons, only one other series went to a seventh game.

In 1993, the Bulls had to beat the Knicks in the Eastern Conference Finals. That series took six games and included two of Jordan's best playoff performances. After losing the first two games of the series at Madison Square Garden, the Bulls came home and dominated the rest of the series. Jordan scored 54 points in Game 4 and followed that up with a triple-double (29–10–14) in Game 5.

With Jordan playing baseball, the Knicks took advantage and eliminated the Bulls in seven games in the second round of the 1994 Eastern Conference playoffs.

During his regular-season career, Jordan scored 1,894 points in 60 games against the Knicks. He scored more points against only Atlanta, Cleveland, Indiana, and Milwaukee. In 27 postseason games against the Knicks, Jordan averaged 33.1 points, 6.4 rebounds, and 6 assists. Jordan also had two career postseason triple-doubles against the Knicks—the only two triple-doubles of MJ's postseason career.

The Bulls and Knicks did not get along.

REPEAT CHAMPS

IN THE 1992 NBA Finals, the Bulls lined up against the team that had passed on Michael Jordan with the second overall pick in the draft, the Portland Trail Blazers. Clyde Drexler had finished fourth in the league in scoring that season, and the Blazers lost only four games in their three series en route to the Finals.

Game 1 saw Jordan put on a shooting display the likes of which we had never seen before. Jordan made only 27 percent of his three-point attempts during the 1991–92 season. But he put that to bed early in the Finals.

Jordan made a then–NBA Finals record six three-pointers in the first half, keying a 57–23 run by the Bulls that blew the doors off the Chicago Stadium and effectively buried the Blazers. When Jordan hit No. 6, he looked at the scorers' table and shrugged—a move that became legendary.

Chicago took Game 1 by 33 points, led by 39 from Jordan. Michael matched his point production in Game 2, but Portland rallied and won by 11 in Chicago.

The series returned to Portland, and the Bulls overcame a 32-point performance from Drexler to win Game 3. Portland held serve in Game 4, led by Jerome Kersey's second of three double-digit rebound games in the series.

Game 5 would be the turning point in the series. With three consecutive games in Portland, the Bulls couldn't lose two of three and come home trailing in the series. Jordan did what he always did—he took over. Michael scored 46 to bring the Bulls home needing one win for a second ring.

Game 6 saw the Blazers take a 15-point lead into the fourth quarter at the Chicago Stadium. Again, Jordan had no intention of going to a Game 7. Chicago outscored Portland 33–14 in the fourth quarter and won their second championship in front of their home fans.

Jordan and Drexler before they were teammates for the USA

1992

THE DREAM TEAM

AFTER WINNING THE 1992 NBA championship, Michael Jordan and Scottie Pippen had time for a quick breather before trying to win another tournament. This time, it was in Barcelona as members of the first United States Olympic team that included NBA players.

The roster was put together controversially by Pistons' head coach Chuck Daly, who did not include his own point guard, Isiah Thomas, in the final group. Every NBA player on the roster was eventually inducted into the Naismith Memorial Basketball Hall of Fame, and "The Dream Team" was inducted as a group as well.

Jordan and Pippen were now teammates with Clyde Drexler, whom they had just defeated for an NBA title. They were also joined by the two elder statesmen of the game, Magic Johnson and Larry Bird. Charles Barkley, Karl Malone, John Stockton, David Robinson, Chris Mullin, Patrick Ewing, and Christian Laettner were also on the roster.

The beginning of the tournament was surreal for the Dream Team. They beat Angola 116–48, and some of their opponents were asking for photos and autographs during the game.

Barkley led the Dream Team in scoring in the tournament, averaging 18 points per game. Jordan led the USA squad in minutes played per game (23.1), field goal attempts per game (14.1), and steals per game (4.1). Jordan finished second to Barkley in scoring (14.9 points per game) and third behind Magic and Pippen in assists (4.8 per game) for the tournament.

The Dream Team were like the Beatles; they couldn't go anywhere without a crowd. The NBA produced a documentary in 2012 about the team's experience in Barcelona that provides an excellent, behind-the-scenes look at the way the team bonded during the tournament.

The 1992 Olympics made Jordan a global superstar. Nike ran ads all over television broadcasts and in the streets in Barcelona with his likeness. His personal brand was elevated from being a basketball star in the United States to a global phenomenon by the end of the Games.

It also made clear to the basketball world in the NBA that Jordan had supplanted Magic and Bird as the king of the game.

However, the game Jordan and Pippen had circled on the schedule in group play was against Croatia and their star forward Toni Kukoč. For a couple years, Jordan and Pippen had heard Jerry Krause talking about how Kukoč was going to be a star in the NBA. They locked him down and took that personally when they faced him.

No team came within 30 points of the Dream Team, which beat Kukoč and Croatia a second time in the gold medal game. Over the eight games in the tournament, the United States out-scored their opponents 938–588 and grabbed 108 more rebounds than the opposition.

The team that changed basketball history across the globe

The Bulls were almost unstoppable for a third-straight season.

1993

REGULAR-SEASON DOMINANCE

THE 1992–93 NBA season started after a short summer for Michael Jordan and Scottie Pippen. Their play during the regular season gave no indication that they were tired, though.

Jordan's scoring average was up by more than two points per game to 32.6, and he won the league scoring title again. He also led the league in steals, averaging 2.8 per game. Pippen was named an NBA All-Star for the third time and led the team in assists while averaging a career-best 7.7 rebounds per game as well.

This season saw point guard B. J. Armstrong come into his own. He established career highs in points (12.3) and assists (4.0) per game and saw his time on the court increase by almost eight minutes per game. He also led the league in three-point shooting percentage that season (45.3 percent).

Horace Grant continued his improvement as well. He finished the regular season fourth in the NBA with 341 offensive rebounds. Jordan, Pippen, Grant, and Armstrong were the only four Bulls players to average in double figures in scoring on one of the league's top offensive units.

Chicago sprinted to a strong start once again, winning six of their first seven games. When the calendar flipped to 1993, the Bulls were 21–7 and had lost consecutive games only once (November 28 at the Knicks and December 2 at the Celtics). Jordan was named the NBA Player of the Month in November.

The Bulls wrapped a seven-game winning streak around the end of the calendar year, not losing a game between December 19 and January 5. The Bulls played 15 games in January and suffered back-to-back losses on three occasions to start the new year. However, they scored at least 120 points in five of the 15 games. Chicago went 6–7 in the month.

February was a different story. The Bulls went 10–2 in the month and won their first five games, all on the road, to close the longest road trip of the season. The Bulls closed the month winning five straight en route to a seven-game streak that ended with an overtime loss in San Antonio on March 5.

Chicago put together another six-game winning streak in the middle of March and a five-game winning streak in April. They finished the regular season with a 57–25 record and won the Central Division for a third consecutive season.

The Bulls were a complete team. They finished second in the NBA with 15.7 offensive rebounds per game (Detroit averaged 15.8). They ranked sixth in the NBA in assists per game (26.0), fifth in the league in steals per game (9.5) and had the fewest turnovers in the league (13.5 per game).

Jordan and Pippen were both named to the NBA's All-Defensive First Team, and Grant was named to the All-Defensive Second Team. Somehow, Pippen was only named to the All-NBA Third Team for the season.

The Chicago Stadium was packed for every game. The Bulls averaged 18,528 and drew a total of 759,656 fans to their 41 home games, which ranked sixth in the NBA.

1993

Michael and the regular-season MVP chatting during the Finals

THREE-PEAT

MAYBE THE VOTERS had Michael Jordan Fatigue, if there could be such a thing. The Phoenix Suns winning an NBA-best 62 regular-season games undoubtedly played a big role. But for those Suns, the worst thing that could have happened was Charles Barkley being named the 1992–93 NBA MVP.

All that did was motivate Jordan even more to win a third consecutive championship.

The Suns won their three playoff series before the NBA Finals, but each series was tough. They lost two games to the Lakers and Spurs in the first two rounds before going the distance with the Sonics in the Western Conference Finals. The Bulls, on the other hand, lost two games total on their way to the Finals.

Jordan and Barkley were two of the biggest names and personalities in the game at the time. They had been teammates on the Dream Team the previous summer. But this was about the ring.

And Jordan wasn't letting Barkley get one on his watch.

Michael scored at least 40 points in four of the six games in the series, including 55 in a stunning Game 4 performance at the Chicago Stadium. Jordan's 41 points per game was the highest average of his six NBA Finals appearances; he also averaged 8.5 rebounds and 6.3 assists per game.

Scottie Pippen played arguably his best Finals series of the Bulls' first three championships as well, averaging 21.2 points, 9.2 rebounds, and 7.7 assists in the series.

But it wasn't Jordan or Pippen who put the final nail in the coffin. It was John Paxson, who knocked down a game-winning three to keep the series from requiring a seventh and decisive game.

The three-peat was complete. The Bulls were a dynasty. And Jordan claimed his third consecutive NBA Finals MVP Award at the expense of Barkley.

JUNE 20
1993

PAX FOR THE WIN

WHEN THE BULLS inbounded the ball with 14.1 seconds remaining in Game 6 of the 1993 NBA Finals, they were trailing by two points in Phoenix. The Suns had stormed back to take a lead, and the Bulls' offense had gone cold. Chicago had nine points in the fourth quarter—and they were all from Michael Jordan.

Jordan was forced to give the ball up prematurely as he crossed center court. And the Suns' defense kept Scottie Pippen from driving to the hoop for a game-tying attempt.

Pippen dropped the ball off to Horace Grant, who also saw his path to the rim disappear. Grant kicked the ball out to John Paxson, who was all alone outside the three-point line. Paxson elevated and released, and the ball found nothing but the bottom of the net with 3.9 seconds remaining on the clock.

Paxson raised both arms to the sky as he retreated to the Bulls bench. Phoenix wasn't able to answer, and the Bulls claimed their third championship in as many seasons.

The shot became one of the iconic moments in the Bulls' dynasty.

Paxson knocked down the biggest shot of his career.

LIFE WITHOUT MIKE

THE 1993-94 REGULAR season was a transition for the Chicago Bulls. Michael Jordan had retired, but the core was still there from three championship teams. It was now up to Scottie Pippen to take the lead. And at 28, he was ready for the bright lights.

The Bulls moved the ball more without Jordan, finishing the season third in the NBA in assists as a team (27.8 per game). They also ranked sixth in the league in total rebounds (46.7 per game) and sixth in steals per game (9.8 per game).

Pippen averaged a career-best 22 points and 8.7 rebounds per game. He also averaged 5.6 assists and 2.9 steals with Jordan away. He played well enough to finish third in MVP voting behind Hakeem Olajuwon and David Robinson—ahead of Shaquille O'Neal.

Pippen closed the regular season being named the NBA's Player of the Month in April. He was named All-NBA First Team, NBA All-Defensive First Team. Pippen finished the season third in the NBA with 211 steals and fourth in player efficiency rating—behind centers Robinson, O'Neal, and Olajuwon. He led the Bulls in scoring, assists and steals.

Horace Grant also elevated his game. He averaged 15.1 points and 11.0 rebounds per game, finished fourth in the league averaging 4.4 offensive rebounds per game, and was named to the NBA All-Defensive Second Team. Pippen, Grant, and Armstrong represented the Bulls in the NBA All-Star Game. And Kukoč was named to the NBA's All-Rookie Second Team.

Only three players appeared in all 82 regular-season games for the Bulls: B. J. Armstrong, Pete Myers, and Steve Kerr. Pippen missed 10 games and Grant missed 12 during the season. Pippen, Grant, and Armstrong were the only Bulls to average more than 25 minutes per game; all three were over 33 minutes per night. Myers joined Pippen, Grant, and Armstrong as the fourth Bulls player to average more than 10 points per game for the season.

A reminder that this was a different era of NBA basketball: Kerr appeared in all 82 games and averaged 24.8 minutes per game. But he attempted only 1.5 three-point attempts per game.

Even without Jordan in the lineup every night, the Bulls still ranked seventh in the NBA in attendance.

The team slowly adjusted to life without No. 23. After starting the season 8–8, Chicago won 10 straight games in December and started to look like the Chicago Bulls. They also rolled off a seven-game winning streak in January, improving to 28–11.

The Bulls finished the regular season 55–27 and second in the Central Division. They went on to sweep the Cleveland Cavaliers in the first round of the playoffs before facing the New York Knicks.

Without Jordan, the Bulls didn't have enough to beat New York. The series went seven games and Pippen led Chicago, averaging 21.7 points and 7.7 rebounds per game.

Unfortunately for Pippen, that series is most remembered for what should have been an exciting moment for the franchise. The Bulls lost the first two games of the series. With the game tied and 1.8 seconds remaining in regulation, Phil Jackson drew up a play for Tony Kukoč—not Pippen. Scottie checked himself out of the game; Kukoč hit the game-winner as the clock expired.

The Knicks would go on to lose to Olajuwon's Rockets in the NBA Finals. And Pippen was forced to answer questions about that play for the rest of his career.

Pippen became the leader when Jordan retired.

BULLS
33
NEW YORK
4
NBC
GAME

PIPPEN'S TIME TO SHINE

Without Mike, Pippen stood as a bona fide star in his own right.

THE 1994 NBA All-Star Game was held in Minneapolis and served as a national coming-out party for Scottie Pippen. He fully emerged from Michael Jordan's shadow in the first game without MJ available for the Eastern Conference Lineup.

The rosters were still loaded with future Hall of Famers.

Pippen was joined on the Eastern Conference roster by Shaquille O'Neal, Patrick Ewing, and Dominique Wilkins. The Bulls and Knicks had three players each; B. J. Armstrong started with Pippen, and Horace Grant came off the bench. Ewing, John Starks and Charles Oakley represented the Knicks—all off the bench. New Jersey's Kenny Anderson and Derrick Coleman started with Pippen, Armstrong, and O'Neal.

The Western Conference was headlined by Hakeem Olajuwon and Utah's tandem of John Stockton and Karl Malone. Clyde Drexler, David Robinson, and Gary Payton also went on to become Hall of Famers; Shawn Kemp and Mitch Richmond started for the West with Olajuwon, Malone, and Drexler.

At the end of the day, Pippen was the game's leading scorer with 29 points. With 11 rebounds also on his line in the box score, Pippen was named the All-Star Game MVP.

1994

JORDAN ON THE DIAMOND

IN 1994, SPORTS fans had a chance to watch Michael Jordan play . . . baseball.

After the tragic death of his father, Jordan walked away from the NBA on top of the mountain to pursue one of his other childhood passions. He signed on with the Birmingham Barons, a minor-league affiliate of the Chicago White Sox.

Jordan had taken a few swings in the batting cage at Comiskey Park while playing for the Bulls, one instance of which was highlighted on a baseball card in 1991. And, on April 7, 1994, Jordan played in what was then known as the Crosstown Classic between Cubs and White Sox prospects. He hit a clutch, game-tying double at Wrigley Field that day.

In the minors, Jordan struggled. But let's be honest: hitting a baseball is the hardest thing to do in professional sports. While his batting average was only .202 in 127 games that summer, Jordan did hit 17 doubles and three home runs. He scored 46 runs with 51 runs batted in as a right fielder. He also stole 30 bases.

You might be able to find an old *Sports Illustrated* with Jordan in a black baseball jersey somewhere online still today. And there were comments made about Jordan playing baseball in the movie *Space Jam* as well.

Minor league outfielder Michael Jordan

1994

The United Center became the new home for the Bulls and Blackhawks.

A NEW HOME

THE END OF the 1993–94 season was bittersweet for Chicago sports fans. The Bulls and Blackhawks were moving into a new home: the United Center. On August 18, 1994, a ribbon-cutting ceremony was held to christen the new home of the two marquee winter sports teams.

There was some controversy with the new building as well. The two teams broke ground to begin building the replacement for the Chicago Stadium in 1992, and Michael Jordan said he didn't want to play anywhere else in his career.

Both the Bulls and Blackhawks moved three championship banners into their new home when they began play. The Bulls' three-peat in the early 1990s soon continued with another three-peat in the new building after Jordan returned. Similarly, the Blackhawks have doubled their number of banners since moving into the new arena.

Since its opening, many improvements to the fan experience have been made. The stadium now includes a sportsbook, new restaurant options, and the atrium area which has the team story, offices, media studios, and an open space that now houses the most famous statue in the city of Chicago.

Unveiling the iconic statue in Chicago

A STATUE FIT FOR THE KING

WHEN THE UNITED Center officially opened for business in August of 1994, it did so without Michael Jordan playing on the new court for the Bulls. But that didn't mean his image wouldn't be present at the new stadium.

The Bulls announced they would erect a statue for Jordan outside the United Center while he was playing baseball. Omri and Julie Rotblatt-Amrany were awarded the design for the statue in January 1994 by the Bulls, and they went to work capturing Jordan in a way that honored and celebrated his career to that point.

On November 1, 1994, the Bulls held a nationally televised celebration of Jordan's career that included Jordan, Jerry Reinsdorf, and Larry King. As part of that event, the Bulls retired Jordan's No. 23 (for the first time) and unveiled the statue titled "The Spirit," which has come to be known simply as The Jordan Statue.

The statue's base lists Jordan's statistical accomplishments and the following quote from the movie *A River Runs Through It*: "At that moment I knew, surely and clearly, that I was witnessing perfection. He stood before us, suspended above the earth, free from all its laws like a work of art, and I knew, just as surely and clearly, that life is not a work of art, and that the moment could not last."

In 2017, the Bulls and Blackhawks opened a new atrium adjacent to the east side of the United Center. The Jordan statue was moved into the middle of the atrium's open area, where it is still regularly visited by fans and tourists for pictures.

APRIL
1995

Jordan and Craig Sager sharing one of many courtside conversations

A NEW LOOK

THE 1994–95 SEASON started for the NBA with the Bulls beginning their second campaign without Michael Jordan. Jordan was playing baseball; the Bulls were trying to find a recipe to return to the top of the Eastern Conference.

Chicago struggled to put together a cohesive offense early in the season. The team was led by Scottie Pippen, but the supporting cast wasn't what it once was. And injuries impacted the roster throughout the season. Only B. J. Armstrong and Steve Kerr appeared in all 82 regular-season contests.

Only Pippen, Toni Kukoč, and Armstrong were averaging in double figures in points per game. Though Pippen was still among the best defensive players in the league, the team defense wasn't what it once was, either.

But there started to be whispers that there may be a return from the franchise's savior. Jordan was having second thoughts about his career choice, and the basketball world was begging for him to come back.

When Jordan returned to the Bulls on March 19 in Indianapolis, the Bulls had won their last three games, but their overall record was only three games over .500 (34–31). In the 17 games in which Jordan appeared to close the regular season, the Bulls went 13–4 to finish third in the Central Division and clinch another playoff berth.

It took a few games for Jordan to get his basketball legs back under him, but he showed flashes of brilliance in his return. He dropped 55 points on the Knicks at the end of March and finished his 17-game regular season averaging 26.9 points, 6.9 rebounds, 5.3 assists, and 1.8 steals per game.

MARCH 19
1995

"I'M BACK"

TICKETS FOR THE Bulls' game at Market Square Arena in Indianapolis might have been the hardest tickets to get at that point in the history of the Bulls' or Pacers' franchises.

The Bulls were three games over .500 coming into the game, and the Pacers were 14 games better than breaking even. It was a rivalry game for certain, and Indy had benefitted from Michael Jordan stepping away from professional basketball to play minor league baseball.

But that man was no longer on the diamond. Michael Jordan was back.

Wearing No. 45—because the Bulls had not yet cleared un-retiring his number with the NBA—Jordan took the court for the first time in almost two years. He played 43 minutes but understandably struggled from the floor; he made just seven of 28 shot attempts.

Jordan scored 19 points, and the Bulls lost the game 103-96. Scottie Pippen led the Bulls—as he had so many times while Jordan was working on hitting fastballs—with 31 points that night.

While the Pacers celebrated the win, the entire NBA was put on notice that the Bulls were coming. Jordan was back where he belonged—on the basketball court.

Michael returned—but without his normal number.

MAY 1995

A talented Magic team got past the Bulls.

A POSTSEASON LOSS

THE BULLS STARTED the 1995 postseason with maybe more confidence than any 5 seed in NBA history. They had Michael Jordan back in the lineup. Even though the rest of the roster had struggled at times during the regular season, having 23 back in the starting lineup was the ultimate game-changer.

Chicago started the playoffs in Charlotte against a good, young Hornets team. Led by Alonzo Mourning, the Hornets presented a difficult matchup.

But the confidence the Bulls had only grew when Jordan scored 48 in the first game in Charlotte. He followed that performance with 32 points in Game 2, but the Hornets won by 17. The Bulls took control of the series with a dominant, 23-point win in Game 3 at the United Center and advanced with a one-point win in the series-clinching fourth game.

That brought a matchup with the young, cocky Orlando Magic. And a familiar face was on the other side: Horace Grant.

The Magic talked the talk going into that series, and their young stars—Shaquille O'Neal and Penny Hardaway—backed it up with their play. The Bulls and Magic split the first two games in Orlando; Jordan scored 38 in Game 2 to lead the Bulls to a 10-point win.

Chicago couldn't match Orlando's size inside, and the Magic's depth was superior as well. Orlando had three players average at least 18 points per game—O'Neal, Hardaway, and Grant—and both O'Neal and Grant averaged at least 11 rebounds per game.

A Jordan turnover in Game 6 sealed the series for the Magic, and the Bulls were eliminated in six games. Orlando players talked like this was their turn to run the Eastern Conference, and that Jordan's time had passed. They went on to get swept by Hakeem Olajuwon and the Houston Rockets in the NBA Finals, Houston's second straight championship.

And their talk about Jordan being the past was a mistake.

"Air Jordan" wearing a number other than 23 never looked quite right.

A once unthinkable duo: Jordan and Rodman in Chicago

THE WORM

VERY RARELY DOES a player universally hated by a city end up playing there and becoming a fan favorite. In Chicago, the Blackhawks acquired enforcer Bob Probert after he had terrorized their players for years with the Red Wings. In 1995, the Bulls added an enforcer who had been a nightmare on behalf of Detroit as well.

On October 2, 1995, the unthinkable happened: The Bulls acquired forward Dennis Rodman, aka The Worm, in a trade for Will Perdue.

To say Rodman's time in San Antonio was a disaster might be an understatement. He was an overwhelming personality contradiction to David Robinson, and the two were never able to comfortably coexist in the Spurs lineup. But the Spurs still wanted someone to support The Admiral in the paint and felt Perdue would do that for them.

Would—could—Rodman coexist with Jordan and Pippen? They had exchanged blows for years during the heat of the Bulls–Pistons rivalry; the word *hate* was absolutely appropriate. But Jordan and Pippen wanted to win, and they knew Rodman was the best defensive power forward in the league.

The Worm led the league in rebounding in all three of his seasons with the Bulls, averaging better than 15 boards per game in 199 regular-season games with Chicago. Yes, there were the trips to Vegas and appearances at wrestling matches. But he was a huge part of the Bulls' dominance during their second three-peat.

1996

THE GREATEST SEASON EVER

WHEN THE 1995–96 NBA regular season began, the refurbished Chicago Bulls were on a mission to prove they—with Michael Jordan—were back. And they took that mission on the court every single night, putting together the best regular season in NBA history.

After a win against Utah on December 23, the Bulls record stood at an astounding 23–2. Their only losses at that point in the season were against Orlando, on whom they would exact revenge in the postseason, and in Seattle, who they would face in the NBA Finals.

The Bulls lost in Indy the day after Christmas. They wouldn't lose again until February 4 in Denver, their fourth game in six nights on the road against good Rockets, Kings, Lakers, and Nuggets teams. On February 2, the Bulls had a ridiculous 41–3 record before traveling to Denver.

The season included an 18-game winning streak and the best road record ever (33–8). If that's not impressive enough, the Bulls only lost two of their 41 home games during the regular season.

Chicago became the first team in NBA history to win 70 games when they defeated the Milwaukee Bucks 86–80 on April 16. That accomplishment broke the record of 69 victories established by the 1971–72 Los Angeles Lakers. Chicago finished the regular season with 72 wins, a number that was eclipsed by the 2015–16 Golden State Warriors (73–9).

For his part, Jordan showed the league he was fully back with a stellar regular season of his own. Vintage Michael returned to lead the NBA in scoring at 30.4 points per game. Dennis Rodman led the league in rebounding (14.9 per game).

Jordan and Scottie Pippen were named First-Team All-NBA. Jordan, Pippen, and Rodman were all named to the NBA's All-Defensive First Team. And Jordan and Pippen started the All-Star Game together for the first time since before Jordan's first retirement.

Benny the Bull celebrating history

1996

Kukoč lived up to the hype with the Bulls.

KUKOČ HONORED

THE BULLS' RELATIONSHIP with Croatian forward Toni Kukoč was a complex long game that paid off.

When Chicago traded veteran Dave Corzine to the Orlando Magic in 1989 for two future second-round picks, it didn't make waves. When the Bulls selected Kukoč with the first of those picks in 1990, it was interesting. But whether or not he would ever come over to North America was a question.

In the years after he was acquired, Kukoč became a bit of an urban legend inside the Bulls organization. General manager Jerry Krause talked him up around the veteran players so much that he was a target of Jordan and Pippen in the 1992 Summer Olympics.

Kukoč finally arrived in the NBA as a 25-year-old in 1993 and started to show why Krause had so much faith. Without Jordan in the lineup, he had a role off the bench and performed well. His scoring average jumped to 15.7 in his second season, and Jordan returned late that season from his baseball hiatus.

When the Bulls sprinted to the best regular-season record in NBA history during the 1995–96 season, Kukoč played a critical role off the bench. His scoring took a step back; bringing Michael back was going to take shots away. But he was good enough to become the first player in Bulls' history to be named the NBA's Sixth Man of the Year.

Kukoč appeared in 436 games for the Bulls over seven seasons. He became an influential player in the emergence of European players coming over and succeeding in the NBA as well. In 2021, Kukoč was inducted into the Naismith Memorial Basketball Hall of Fame.

1996

COACH OF THE YEAR

WHEN YOU WIN a league-record 72 games, postseason awards tend to come your way. And the Chicago Bulls received their due in the league's postseason honors after their history-making 1995–96 season.

But the one award that stands out wasn't given to a player.

The Bulls won three championships in the decade before the 1995–96 season, but the league had honored Don Cheney, Don Nelson, and Pat Riley with the league's Coach of the Year award in those three seasons. Even while Michael Jordan was playing baseball, the league overlooked the Bulls and gave the league's top coaching honor to Lenny Wilkins and Del Harris.

Chicago hadn't had the NBA's Coach of the Year since Dick Motta after the 1970–71 season. But the league couldn't ignore Phil Jackson any longer.

Following their record-breaking season, Jackson was named the NBA's Coach of the Year for the only time while he was with the Bulls. In fact, even with the success he enjoyed coaching the Lakers in the years following his departure from Chicago, Jackson never won the Coach of the Year award again.

Lead the best team in history? Yeah, that's Coach of the Year stuff.

RUNAWAY MVP

AFTER A LONG summer without baseball, Michael Jordan returned with a vengeance for the 1995–96 regular season. In the season's opening game, he scored 42 points with six boards and seven assists.

That was only a taste of what was to come.

Jordan was back on the floor and back on his game. He led the league in scoring at 30.4 points per game. He added 6.6 rebounds, 4.3 assists, and 2.2 steals per game, appearing in all 82 games in the regular season. And he did all of that in 37.7 minutes per game, his lightest work load since the 1990–91 season.

Of course, when the team around him is loaded with great players and on its way to winning an NBA-record 72 games, the minutes required from the best player weren't as heavy.

The signature game of the season for Jordan came against Detroit on March 7. In 38 minutes of action, Jordan scored 53 points on 21 of 28 shooting from the field and nine of 10 from the line. He added 11 rebounds, two assists, and six steals in a 102–81 victory.

Jordan was named the NBA's Most Valuable Player for the fourth time following the Bulls' triumphant 1995–96 season. He received 109 of 113 first-place votes; only Hakeem Olajuwon, Anfernee Hardaway, and Karl Malone also received first-place votes that year.

How good were the Bulls that season? Scottie Pippen finished fifth in MVP voting, and Dennis Rodman also appeared on ballots (he finished 15th in voting).

But the award went to Michael, who was ready to show the world—and, especially, the Orlando Magic—that his time had in fact not passed.

Jordan soared back to his usual greatness and took home another MVP.

An emotional Michael Jordan reacting to another championship victory

BACK ON TOP

THE 1996 NBA Finals stacked up as what could have been the toughest test of any of the Bulls' championship series. Seattle's Gary Payton was named the league's Defensive Player of the Year, and Shawn Kemp was one of the most ferocious offensive players in the league. George Karl led the Sonics to a 64–18 record, the second-best mark in the entire NBA.

In many years, 64 wins would have been the best in the league. Unfortunately for the Sonics, the Bulls won 72 that year. And they were looking for redemption after an early dismissal from the previous year's postseason.

The Bulls swept the Miami Heat in the first round and lost just one of five games against the Knicks in the second. That set up the matchup everyone wanted in the Eastern Conference Finals: Bulls versus Magic. And nobody in the Bulls' dressing room forgot the talk from the year before.

Michael Jordan averaged 29.5 points per game in the conference finals. Scottie Pippen averaged 18.5 points, 7.3 rebounds, and 7 assists per game. And Dennis Rodman haunted Shaquille O'Neal; The Worm averaged 11.5 points and 15.8 rebounds. Chicago swept the Magic and advanced to face Seattle.

The Bulls sprinted to a 3–0 series lead with Rodman dominating the glass. In the years that followed, many have questioned why Karl waited until the fourth game of the series to put his best defensive option, Payton, on Jordan. When he did, the Sonics won the next two games.

But on Sunday, June 16—Father's Day—the Bulls were back on their home court, and Michael wasn't one to allow a series to go the distance. The Bulls won the clinching game by 12, and Jordan was named the series MVP.

It was significant that the clinching game came on Father's Day for Michael. This was his first championship without his father, James. In the moments after the final buzzer sounded, he collapsed on the court, clenching the game ball crying.

Ultimately, it was the Bulls' depth that was the difference in the series. Five Seattle players averaged in double figures in points per game in the series; no other player on their roster averaged better than 2.8 points per game. Nine Bulls players averaged at least that number. The Bulls also had seven players average at least 18.8 minutes per game in the series. And the Bulls averaged nearly five assists per game more than the Sonics.

That depth and the Bulls' defensive greatness was never more evident than in the final game of the series. Only three Seattle players—Detlef Schrempf, Kemp, and Payton—scored more than seven points. The Bulls held Sam Perkins to 3 of 14 shooting and out-rebounded the Sonics 51–35 in the clinching effort.

Seattle may have come up short in the Finals, but Kemp established himself as a bona fide superstar. He led the Sonics averaging 23.3 points, 10 rebounds and two blocked shots per game. Payton averaged 18 points, seven assists, and 1.5 steals per game in the series as well.

The Bulls were a balanced team in their fourth championship series. Four Bulls—Jordan, Scottie Pippen, Toni Kukoč, and Luc Longley— averaged double-digit points in the series. Dennis Rodman averaged 14.7 rebounds per game. Pippen was excellent, averaging a team-leading 5.3 assists and 2.5 steals per game. And Longley led the team averaging 1.8 blocks per game.

KERR FROM DOWNTOWN

DURING THE 1994–95 season, guard Steve Kerr emerged as a legit three-point threat for the Bulls. He led the NBA from deep, shooting 52.4 percent from beyond the line.

At the 1997 NBA All-Star Weekend in Cleveland, Kerr was looking to win the Three-Point Contest for the first time in three tries. He was up against a tough field that included Hall of Famer John Stockton, Tim Legler (the previous year's champion), Dale Ellis, Glen Rice, Terry Mills, Sam Perkins, and Walt Williams.

Kerr scored 15 points in the first round of the contest, making him the fourth of four players to make the semifinals. From there, he was unstoppable. Kerr scored 21 in the semifinals, the top score in the round. He faced Legler in the final and beat him by a score of 22–18.

That victory is often forgotten in discussions of Kerr's 1996–97 season because of the game-winning shot he hit in Game 6 of the NBA Finals to beat the Utah Jazz and clinch the Bulls' fifth NBA championship.

The win made Kerr the first Bulls player to win the Three-Point Contest since Craig Hodges won three in a row from 1990 to 1992. Kerr is still the last Bulls player to win the event three decades later.

In recent years, Kerr has led arguably the greatest three-point shooting team in the history of the NBA as the head coach of the Golden State Warriors. So his winning the NBA's Three-Point Contest is a fascinating moment to consider in the history of the league.

Over his 15-year NBA career—during which he was a five-time NBA champion—Kerr shot the greatest percentage on three-point attempts of any player in league history (45.4 percent). He led the league in that category twice in his career, making 50.7 percent in 1989–90 with the Cavs and 52.4 percent in 1994–95 with the Bulls. However, he only attempted 1.8 three-pointers per game in 910 career appearances. He attempted 1,599 total three pointers in his career.

During the 1996–97 NBA season, teams across the league averaged 16.8 three-point attempts per game. Only five teams—the Heat, Rockets, Hawks, Nuggets, and Magic—averaged more than 20 attempts from deep per game. And the league collectively shot 36 percent from downtown.

Comparatively, the league attempted 62.5 two-point shots per game that season and made 48 percent of their shots.

During the 2024–25 NBA season, NBA teams collectively averaged 37.6 three-point attempts per game. The lowest average in the league was Denver, who put up "only" 31.9 three-pointers per game. The league made the exact same 36 percent from deep nearly 30 years later. Kerr's Warriors were second in the league, averaging 42.4 three-pointers per game.

However, the NBA attempted only 51.7 two-point shots per game during the 2024–25 campaign and made 54.5 percent.

Kerr's star player while coaching with the Warriors, Steph Curry, has made an NBA record 4,058 three-pointers as of the end of the 2024–25 regular season. That total is almost 900 more than any player in league history (James Harden is second with 3,175). Curry has attempted 9,589 three-pointers. Meanwhile, Kerr's 726 made three-pointers doesn't even make the all-time top 250 in league history.

Long before coaching Steph Curry, Steve Kerr was lethal from deep.

DEFENDING GREATNESS

AFTER THEIR RIDICULOUS, historic, 72-win season and subsequent championship, the Bulls returned to the hardwood for the 1996–97 season back on top of the NBA mountain. And they once again had a target on them from the start of the season.

Could they match their previous success, though? Many fans and media analysts thought it was possible.

The Bulls did nothing to dismiss those beliefs; they won their first 12 games of the regular season. After a loss in Utah, they then rolled off five more in a row. With a win over the Pistons on Christmas Day, the Bulls were 24–3.

Chicago had three win streaks of at least seven games in the second half of the season and finished the year with 69 victories. They won the Central Division by 13 games; Atlanta finished second. The only other team in the Eastern Conference that won more than 57 games was the Miami Heat, who won 61.

The Bulls were the top-scoring team in the Eastern Conference; they were the only team to average more than 101 points per game (103.1). And only three teams in the conference—Miami, Atlanta, and Detroit—allowed fewer points per game than the Bulls (92.3).

Michael Jordan led the league in scoring, averaging 29.6 points per game. Dennis Rodman led the league in rebounding, averaging 16.1 boards per night. Jordan and Scottie Pippen were both on the NBA's All-Defensive First Team, while Jordan was First-Team All-NBA and Pippen was Second-Team All-NBA.

One individual honor that did not come to the Bulls was the league's Most Valuable Player, however. That was bestowed on Utah's Karl Malone, who led the Jazz to the best record in the Western Conference (64–18).

Jordan, Pippen, and Rodman formed a dominant defensive force together.

Five trophies in seven years

RING NO. 5

JUST AS THEY had in 1993, voters for the NBA's awards did a tremendous disservice to a future Hall of Famer by naming him—and not Michael Jordan—the league's Most Valuable Player. Karl Malone had a terrific 1996–97 campaign, averaging 27.4 points and 9.9 rebounds per game for what many might argue was the best team in Utah Jazz history. He barely edged out Jordan for the MVP; Malone received 63 first place votes to 52 for Jordan.

As he usually did, Jordan took that personally. And when he got a chance to show the world who was the real MVP in the 1997 NBA Finals, Jordan made sure to put his mark on the series.

The Bulls won the first two games at the United Center before travelling to Utah. To his credit, Malone was exceptional in the series and elevated his game when the series travelled west. The Jazz took the first two games in Utah with the Mailman leading the game in scoring in both contests.

Michael offered a legendary performance in Game 5, and the Bulls came home with a chance to close the series. Jordan left no doubt in the clinching game, scoring 39 points and claiming his fifth NBA Finals MVP trophy.

Only three players in the series averaged at least 20 points per game. Scottie Pippen averaged 20 points and a team-leading 8.3 rebounds per game. Malone averaged 23.8 points—below his season average—and 10.3 rebounds per game in the series. Dennis Rodman annoyed Malone the entire series and averaged 7.7 rebounds per game for Chicago.

Jordan's numbers in the series rank among his most complete in any of his NBA Finals series. He averaged 32.3 points, seven rebounds, six assists, and 1.2 steals per game.

JUNE 11
1997

THE FLU GAME

AMONG ALL THE remarkable performances in the incredible career of Michael Jordan, perhaps no individual game stands out as much as Game 5 of the 1997 NBA Finals.

The buzz before the game was about whether or not Jordan was even going to be able to play. He was reportedly sick enough that he was a question mark for the game, receiving fluids all day and arriving to the arena to his usual circus of cameras looking like less than his best.

Chicago needed all of Jordan. The series was tied 2–2 going into a pivotal road game. What we learned years later in *The Last Dance* documentary was that Jordan had food poisoning; he had eaten a questionable pizza in the hotel the night before, and it had taken a toll on him.

With his body drained, everything Jordan did was on camera. He regularly slouched over to collect himself. Scottie Pippen helped him off the floor for timeouts. If you ignored the box score, one might think Jordan wasn't physically able to perform.

When the final horn sounded on a 90–88 Bulls victory in which they erased a five-point deficit in the fourth quarter, Jordan had poured in 38 points with seven rebounds, five assists, and three steals. He scored 15 in the fourth quarter to carry his team to a huge win.

The flu? Bad pizza? Jordan still had just enough to win.

APRIL
1998

THE LAST DANCE

IF YOU'VE SEEN the documentary series *The Last Dance,* you know the Bulls entered the 1997–98 season knowing this might be it for their run of success. A number of key players had contracts coming up at the end of the year, as did head coach Phil Jackson. The end appeared to be near.

After so many dominant starts to seasons during the dynasty years, this time was different. When the Bulls hosted the Toronto Raptors on December 13, Chicago entered the game with just a 12–9 record. That night started an eight-game win streak that started to show the Bulls meant business once again.

Beginning with the win against the Raptors the Bulls went on a 30–6 tear with two eight-game win streaks included. But two of those six losses were to the Utah Jazz, who the Bulls had defeated in the previous year's NBA Finals.

The Bulls finished the regular season third in the NBA in team defense, allowing only 89.6 points per game. They finished first in the NBA in attendance, seeing almost one million fans come to the United Center to watch them chase a sixth championship.

Michael Jordan won the league scoring title again. Dennis Rodman led the league in rebounding, averaging 15 boards per night. But the league was perhaps as competitive as at any time during the Bulls' dynasty.

Chicago was the only team in the Eastern Conference to win at least 60 games during the regular season, but three teams reached that mark in the West; Utah won 62, and the Sonics and Lakers won 61 games each. The Bulls claimed another Central Division title, but they had their work cut out for them to win a sixth title.

The bond that was created between Michael and Kobe transcended the court.

BULLS
23

The trash talk between Reggie Miller and Michael Jordan was legendary.

GOING THE DISTANCE VS. INDY

AFTER CHICAGO WON seven of their first eight playoff games against the Nets and Hornets, the Indiana Pacers stood between the Bulls and a third straight NBA Finals.

For only the second time during the dynasty years with Jordan on the floor, the Bulls needed seven games to advance.

Over the years, the Pacers had developed into a legitimate Eastern Conference power. They finished the 1997–98 season in second place in the Central Division with Larry Bird calling the shots as their head coach. Indy had easily knocked out the Cavs and Knicks in the first two rounds, losing only one game in each series.

Like the Pistons and Knicks before them, the Pacers played a physical game against the Bulls, and they talked. A lot. With notorious trash-talkers Reggie Miller and Jalen Rose joined by Mark Jackson in their backcourt, the Pacers could dish it out with the best teams in the league.

The Bulls held their home court, winning two close games at the United Center to start the series. But the Pacers won the next two games—also close—in Indy to even the series. Miller hit a game-winning three-pointer with two seconds left to steal an emotional Game 4 in Indianapolis.

The back-and-fourth continued for three more games, with the only easy win coming for the Bulls in Game 5. Only one game in the entire series was decided by more than six points.

In Game 7 the Bulls started Toni Kukoč, and it paid off. The teams traded big swings in the first half and then played nearly even basketball in the second half. Jordan scored 28; Miller scored 22. The difference maker was Kukoč, whose 21 points were huge. The Bulls won the series with an 88–83 victory in Game 7.

The Pacers proved to be a tough opponent for the champs.

1998

Two great champions: Bill Russell and Michael Jordan

ANOTHER MVP

AFTER TWO MORE championships following his return to playing basketball full-time, Michael Jordan entered the 1997–98 regular season with elements of finality hanging over the year. Decisions needed to be made about the roster after that season, and Phil Jackson was calling it their "last dance" from the start of training camp.

Jordan turned 35 in February during the season, but still appeared in all 82-regular season games. His 38.8 minutes per game was his highest average over a full regular season since before his first retirement. But the rest of his numbers were slightly down from the previous season.

Michael still led the league in scoring for the 10th straight season (not including his 17-game return in 1994–95). But his 28.7 point-per-game average was his lowest since his broken foot season in 1985–86. His rebound average (5.8) was his lowest since 1987–88, and his assist average (3.5) was his lowest since 1985–86.

None of that mattered to the voters for the NBA's end-of-season awards. After Karl Malone was named the league's MVP the previous year, Jordan won his fifth and final MVP award. He was also named First-Team All-NBA and All-Defensive First Team. Not a bad season for a guy who turned 35 around the All-Star Game—in which he appeared for the 12th time representing the Bulls.

ANOTHER THREE-PEAT

AFTER THE BULLS beat the Utah Jazz in the NBA Finals in 1997, the two teams performed well enough to run it back for a second straight postseason in 1998. This time, however, the Jazz were coming into the series with home court advantage. Utah tied the Bulls with the best record in the league (62–20) but got to host Game 1 of the Finals.

The Bulls were coming out of just the second seven-game postseason series of the Jordan Era, a win over the Indiana Pacers that was physically grueling. The Jazz, on the other hand, swept the Lakers to advance to the Finals. Utah was well rested and ready.

Despite Michael Jordan scoring 33, the Jazz won Game 1 by three points. Chicago answered with a five-point win in Game 2, taking a tied series back to the United Center.

Game 3 was arguably the greatest defensive performance in the history of the NBA Finals. Karl Malone scored 22 points, but no other Jazz player scored more than eight. The Bulls held the Jazz to 23 points in the second half; Chicago scored at least that many in both the third and fourth quarters.

Led by four steals from Toni Kukoč, the Bulls had 13 as a team and six blocked shots. The final score: 96–54. A completely dominant performance on the Bulls' home floor.

The Bulls won Game 4 in less dominant fashion, setting up a potential clinch scenario on their home floor in Game 5. Led by 39 points from Malone, Utah escaped with a narrow victory to force the series back to their arena.

Jordan always knew how to celebrate.

Game Six was as close as any game can be. Malone was good; Jordan was great. And as he did throughout his illustrious career, Jordan made sure the NBA Finals did not see a seventh game. A late steal from Malone, followed by maybe the most iconic shot in the history of the NBA closed the books on the series—and the Bulls' dynasty.

Jordan averaged 33.5 points per game and won his sixth NBA Finals MVP.

DYNASTY DISMANTLED

WHEN THE CONFETTI had been cleaned up and the parade was over for the Bulls' sixth championship in eight years, what was called the "Last Dance" by Phil Jackson—which became the name of a stellar documentary series about that season—was over. Sadly, the dynasty was about to implode.

Ten Bulls players and Jackson were unsigned beyond the 1997–98 season. Complicating matters further was an NBA lockout that began on July 1, and teams couldn't negotiate with players during the labor stoppage.

Three weeks into the lockout the Bulls hired Tim Floyd—but not as head coach (at that point). Jerry Krause named him the president of basketball operations; if Jackson came back, he would report to Floyd. The Bulls had flirted with hiring Floyd for a few years, and Jackson's agent blasted the hiring in the media.

On January 13, 1999, Jordan retired from the Bulls for good. That served as the start of a historic turnover that cast the Bulls from the top to the bottom of the league.

Floyd was officially named the head coach two days later. When the NBA lockout ended on January 20, 1999, the Bulls renounced their rights to Jordan, Dennis Rodman, Joe Kleine, and Jud Buechler. They also traded Steve Kerr to the Spurs.

Two days later, the Bulls traded Scottie Pippen to the Rockets for Roy Rogers and a second-round pick. The day after the Pippen trade, the Bulls traded Luc Longley to the Suns for Mark Bryant, Martin Muursepp, Bubba Wells, and a future first round pick.

Over a span of 10 days, the Bulls completely dismantled their dynasty.

NBA Commissioner David Stern, Michael Jordan, and Jerry Reinsdorf

TIM FLOYD

THE 1997–98 SEASON, which ended with the Chicago Bulls celebrating their sixth NBA championship, was followed by the complete dismantling of the team. Included in the departures was head coach Phil Jackson, a move that was disappointing for fans but expected with the core players all moving on as well.

Looking for a head coach to begin the next generation in Chicago, the Bulls hired Iowa State head coach Tim Floyd to lead the team on January 15, 1999, at the conclusion of the NBA lockout. The introduction of Floyd came just two days after Michael Jordan retired (for a second time) from the Bulls.

The Floyd Era did not go well. Indeed, it was filled with two things: roster turnover and losses. In Floyd's four years as the head coach of the Bulls, his teams posted a 49–190 record (just a .205 winning percentage). He was fired after just 25 games during the 2001–02 season, at which point the Bulls had a 4–21 record.

The Bulls finished in last place in each of the seasons during which Floyd was the head coach.

Floyd had the insurmountable task of replacing Phil Jackson.

STARTING OVER

Elton Brand becomes a Chicago Bull.

THE LOCKOUT-SHORTENED 1998–99 NBA season was brutal for the Bulls. They won only 13 of their 50 games and established an NBA record on April 10, scoring only 49 points in an entire game against the Miami Heat.

Chicago was "rewarded" for their futility with the No. 1 overall pick in the 1999 NBA Draft, the first time the franchise had ever held the top selection. That draft was billed as very good and deep. It was also the first time Duke coach Mike Krzyzewski had ever lost a player to an NBA draft early.

One of the four players who declared for the draft before completing four years at Duke was Elton Brand. He dealt with injuries during his two seasons at Duke but was the consensus top prospect in the draft. So when the Bulls selected Brand first overall, it came as little surprise.

Chicago also owned the 16th overall pick in the 1999 draft, acquired from the Phoenix Suns in the trade that sent center Luc Longley to the desert. With that pick, the Bulls drafted a gritty forward from St. John's named Ron Artest.

The Bulls selected forwards Michael Ruffin and Lari Ketner in the second round of the 1999 draft. Ruffin went on to appear in 414 NBA games. Ketner made 25 appearances in NBA games.

BIG MONEY BRENT

ON JANUARY 25, 1999, the Chicago Bulls officially began their post-Michael Jordan era with a significant signing. Brent Barry, a 27-year-old guard coming off an injury-shortened season that was split between the Clippers and Heat, signed a six-year, $27 million deal. The deal was signed in January as the NBA was coming out of a lockout.

When he learned of the signing, Heat coach Pat Riley sarcastically told the media "If he does well in Chicago then obviously they think they have the next Michael Jordan. Whatever."

Barry had won the NBA Slam Dunk contest as a rookie as a member of the Nuggets, but was traded to the Clippers soon after.

The deal didn't work out for either side. After appearing in 37 games and averaging 12.6 points per game in his first season with Chicago, Barry was traded to the Sonics for James Cotton and Hersey Hawkins.

Barry would go on to win NBA championships in 2005 and 2007 as a member of the San Antonio Spurs.

Brent Barry signed a big contract to join the Bulls.

2000

Elton Brand and Steve Francis shared the Rookie of the Year Award.

CO-ROOKIE OF THE YEAR

BREAKING INTO THE NBA at just 20 years old, Elton Brand was supposed to become the new face of a Bulls franchise that was emerging from the shadow of Michael Jordan. Brand led Duke to the NCAA championship game and was named the consensus National Player of the Year and ACC Player of the Year.

And his rookie season went a long way in making believers of many fans.

Brand put to rest concerns about his college injuries, appearing in 81 games as a rookie. He averaged 20.1 points and 10 rebounds per game, leading the team in both statistical categories. Unfortunately, the Bulls finished the 1999–2000 season with a 17–65 record and in last place in the Eastern Conference.

Even with the team's overall struggles, Brand did enough to earn NBA Co-Rookie of the Year honors. He shared the honor with the No. 2 pick in that year's draft, Houston guard Steve Francis. Brand was also named to the NBA's All-Rookie team.

AUGUST 2
2000

SETTLING FOR MERCER

THE BULLS WERE coming out of a tough span of eight months in which they had signed Brent Barry (who was traded less than two weeks after the Mercer signing) and courted big-name free agents Tracy McGrady, Grant Hill, and Tim Duncan. McGrady and Hill signed with the Orlando Magic while Duncan remained in San Antonio.

On August 2, 2000, the Chicago Bulls signed 24-year-old guard Ron Mercer to a four-year, $27 million deal. The Bulls became the fourth team on Mercer's resume in his first four years of his NBA career despite being named to the NBA's All-Rookie team after the 1997–98 season.

Mercer was originally selected by the Boston Celtics with the sixth overall pick in the 1997 NBA Draft after he helped Kentucky reach the Final Four in each of his two college seasons. He was also an important part of the Wildcats' 1996 NCAA title.

Mercer performed better with the Bulls than Barry; he averaged a career-high 19.7 points per game in 61 games. Unfortunately—like Barry—his time in Chicago was not long. After appearing in 40 games for the Bulls during the 2001–02 season, Mercer was traded to the Indianapolis Pacers in a blockbuster deal.

Ron Mercer wasn't the big-ticket signing the Bulls hoped for.

JUNE 28
2000

DRAFTING THE CRAWSOVER

WHEN THE 2000 NBA Draft arrived, the Chicago Bulls owned six selections. Unfortunately for the Bulls, that year's class wasn't great. But the Bulls did make one move during the draft that brought energy to the United Center.

After Kenyon Martin, Stromile Swift, and Darius Miles were selected with the first three overall picks, the Bulls were on the clock at No. 4 overall. They selected Iowa State power forward Marcus Fizer.

Chicago was back on the clock at No. 7 overall, where they selected Texas center Chris Mihm. Still in the first round, the Bulls picked German center Dalibor Bagarić at No. 24.

The Bulls owned three consecutive picks early in the second round. They selected Indiana guard A. J. Guyton at No. 32 and then UConn teammates center Jake Voskuhl and guard Khalid El-Amin at Nos. 33 and 34, respectively.

Among the six players selected by the Bulls that year, Voskuhl's 450 regular-season games were the most during their NBA careers. But Mihm never played for the Bulls.

During the draft the Bulls sent Mihm to Cleveland in a trade that brought guard Jamal Crawford—whom the Cavaliers had drafted out of Michigan with the eighth overall pick—to Chicago.

Crawford was a dynamic scorer who could get buckets at any time, anywhere. He went on to play 20 years in the NBA, though only the first four were for the Bulls.

Crawford was one of the most offensively dynamic players of his generation.

THE TWIN TOWERS

THE BULLS WERE coming off another season of struggles when the 2001 NBA Draft took place. Chicago owned the No. 4 overall selection and were looking to change the fortunes of the franchise yet again. Ironically, the top pick in the 2001 NBA Draft belonged to the Washington Wizards, for whom Michael Jordan would make the pick.

There were rumors that Elton Brand, who had averaged 20 points and 10 assists per game over his first two seasons in Chicago, wasn't happy; he had won more games his final season at Duke (37) than he did in his first two NBA seasons combined (32). And the Bulls were looking to get more athletic.

So the Bulls traded a player some believed would be a building block for their future, Brand, to the Los Angeles Clippers to acquire the second overall selection. Chicago viewed two high school prospects—local product Eddy Curry and Tyson Chandler—as their future frontcourt. Both were nearly seven feet tall and could move.

The trade didn't work for the Bulls, who spent the next three years near the bottom of the NBA.

Unfortunately, the third overall pick in 2001, Pau Gasol, wouldn't play for the Bulls until much later in his career.

The Bulls went big twice with Eddy Curry and Tyson Chandler.

2001

Former center Cartwright moved from the post to the bench in Chicago.

CARTWRIGHT TAKES OVER

WHEN THE TIM Floyd Era came to a crashing conclusion 27 games into the 2001–02 season, a familiar face took over the head coaching duties for the Bulls.

Bill Cartwright returned to Chicago, where he had won three championships as the center for the Bulls, as an assistant coach on Phil Jackson's staff before the 1996–97 season. He was one of very few individuals who remained after the tear-down that followed the end of the second three-peat, becoming part of Floyd's coaching staff. When Floyd got his pink slip, Cartwright was made the interim head coach.

The roster Cartwright inherited was a mess and finished the 2001–02 season with only 21 wins. Despite that, Cartwright had "interim" removed from his office door; he was made the permanent head coach. The Bulls struggled to a 30–52 mark in the 2002–03 season. When the Bulls started the 2003–04 season 4–10, Cartwright was relieved of his duties on the bench.

Another former Bulls player, Pete Myers, was named the interim coach when Cartwright was fired.

J-WILL

THE TOP OF the 2002 NBA Draft seemed like a lock. The Houston Rockets had the top selection, and used it to select center Yao Ming. He was the first player from China to be selected first overall; he went on to be inducted into the Naismith Memorial Basketball Hall of Fame.

Far from a consolation prize, the Bulls had the second overall pick. They needed a guard to change the direction of their franchise, and the right guy was available. Duke guard Jay Williams, who had had a standout career that included the 2001 NCAA championship and was the 2002 Player of the Year, was coming to Chicago.

Williams had a solid rookie campaign, averaging 9.5 points and 4.7 assists in 75 games. He was named to the NBA's All-Rookie second team, and he looked like he might be the point guard of the future.

Unfortunately, on the night of June 19, 2003, Williams crashed a motorcycle into a streetlight. His injuries were severe and required extensive rehab; the crash also violated his contract with the Bulls. The 2003 NBA Draft was one week later, and the injuries suffered by Williams led to the Bulls looking for his replacement. He never played another NBA game.

Jay Williams becomes a Chicago Bull.

FEBRUARY 19
2002

Fab Five legend Jalen Rose joined the Bulls.

A BLOCKBUSTER TRADE BETWEEN RIVALS

THE BULLS' SEARCH for the right mix of players took a hard turn on February 19, 2002. Chicago had signed guard Ron Mercer and center Brad Miller as free agents during the summer of 2000 with hopes they could lead a turnaround for the franchise, but it never materialized.

Still trying to spark a rejuvenation of the team on the court, the Bulls traded Mercer, Miller, Ron Artest (now known as Metta World Peace), and Kevin Ollie to their division rivals in Indy for Jalen Rose, Travis Best, Norm Richardson, and a second-round pick in the 2002 NBA Draft (which was eventually used to select forward Lonny Baxter).

Rose was the best-known player in the deal; he had been a core member of the University of Michigan's legendary Fab Five team. The trade sent the Pacers two players—Miller and Artest—who emerged as bona fide stars in the deal, while the Bulls were never able to turn the pieces they received into a winning combination.

Rose appeared in 128 games for the Bulls over three seasons before he was traded—with Baxter and Donyell Marshall—to the Toronto Raptors for Antonio Davis, Jerome Williams, and Chris Jeffries.

CAPTAIN KIRK

THE TOP OF the 2003 NBA Draft was loaded with star power. When Cleveland won the draft lottery, they won the right to keep LeBron James in Ohio to start his hyped NBA career. Fans were also salivating over the prospects of selecting Carmelo Anthony, Chris Bosh, or Dwyane Wade.

Many Bulls fans hoped Wade, who played locally in high school and was a star at Marquette, would fall to them at No. 7 overall. Unfortunately, Pat Riley took him off the board with the fifth pick.

After the top five picks, the draft became more of a wild card. After Chris Kaman was selected by the Clippers, the Bulls grabbed Kansas point guard Kirk Hinrich.

Hinrich may not have been a superstar like the four future Hall of Famers at the top of the draft, but he was a solid guard for the Bulls. Even with all the stars in the class, Hinrich was named to the NBA's All-Rookie First Team.

He played for the Bulls over parts of 11 seasons and was the tough-nosed guard the team needed after Jay Williams's accident. He ranks 10th from his draft class in career regular-season games played (879).

Today, Hinrich ranks third in Bulls franchise history in games played (748), fourth in minutes played (24,798), and is the franchise's all-time leader in three-pointers made (1,049). He ranks in the team's all-time top 10 in assists (third, with 3,811), steals (third, with 857), and total points (ninth, with 8,536). He was also named to the All-Defensive second team after the 2006–07 season.

Between 2003 and 2010, Hinrich was a critical part of the Bulls' success. And he's one of the underrated players from the 2003 NBA Draft who went on to have a solid professional career.

Hinrich became a leader in Chicago.

Skiles took over as the bench boss of the Bulls.

COACH SKILES

PETE MYERS SERVED as the Bulls' interim head coach briefly during the 2003–04 season until Chicago named Scott Skiles their new head coach for the final 66 games of that regular season. The Bulls would only win 19 of those 66 contests, but it appeared the Bulls had a coach who could get more out of the players.

In his first full season as the head coach of the Bulls, Chicago improved dramatically. Skiles led the Bulls to a 47–35 mark and back into the playoffs in the 2004–05 season. The Bulls were eliminated in the first round of the Eastern Conference Playoffs in six games. The next year, the Bulls finished with a .500 record but made the playoffs again, only suffer the same six-game result in the first round.

The 2006–07 season saw the Bulls take a significant step forward. They won 49 games during the regular season and swept the Miami Heat in the first round of the playoffs. They ran into the Detroit Pistons in the second round and lost in, you guessed it, six games.

When the Bulls struggled to a 9–16 record to start the 2007–08 season, Skiles was removed from the head coaching job.

A REALLY GOOD DRAFT

THE BULLS WERE still reeling from the injury to Jay Williams one year later when the 2004 NBA Draft arrived. It appeared they had found a suitable replacement point guard in Hinrich, but were still trying to build a competitive roster.

Chicago owned the third overall pick in the draft and acquired the seventh overall pick in a trade with the Phoenix Suns. Those two selections would, with Hinrich, help shape the next half-decade of Bulls basketball.

After Orlando selected Dwight Howard first and Charlotte took Emeka Okafor second, the Bulls picked guard Ben Gordon from UConn. With the pick from the Suns, Chicago selected Duke forward Luol Deng.

Both Gordon and Deng were voted NBA All-Rookie First Team players after their rookie season. With Gordon coming off the bench and Deng starting at small forward, the Bulls began to improve.

In five seasons with the Bulls, Gordon averaged 18.5 points per game and was instant offense off the bench. He posted a career-best 21.4 points per game during the 2006–07 season.

Deng played the first ten years of his career in Chicago, averaging 16.1 points and 6.4 rebounds per game. He represented the Bulls in two NBA All-Star Games (2012 and 2013) and was as consistent as they come.

Hinrich, Gordon, and Deng became linked together in Bulls history as three players who turned the franchise back into a contender.

Luol Deng joined the list of Duke players drafted by the Bulls.

GORDON WINS SIXTH MAN OF THE YEAR

THE NBA STARTED recognizing bench excellence formally in the 1982–83 season when they began handing out the Sixth Man of the Year Award. In the 40 years that the hardware has been distributed, only two Chicago Bulls have won the award.

When Ben Gordon won the award at the conclusion of his rookie season, he was the youngest player to win it; he was just 21 at the time. The youngest players to win the award since Gordon—James Harden (2012) and Tyler Herro (2022)—were both 22 at the time.

Gordon burst onto the scene in a supporting role in his first professional season, averaging 15.1 points and shooting 40.5 percent from three-point range.

No game from that rookie season stands out like his virtuoso performance on March 30 against the Hornets in Charlotte. Gordon scored 22 points on 8 of 12 shooting—in the fourth quarter! He scored Chicago's final 16 points and finished with a game-high 35 points in a 102–99 win.

Gordon was lethal off the bench for the Bulls.

DECEMBER 9
2005

Pippen's banner joined Jordan and Jackson in the rafters.

33 TO THE RAFTERS

ON DECEMBER 9, 2005, the Chicago Bulls put Scottie Pippen's No. 33 in the rafters. His banner hangs next to those of Michael Jordan, Phil Jackson, and Jerry Krause as a reminder of the greatness of the dynasty of the 1990s.

The relationship between the Bulls and Pippen was tumultuous throughout his career. There were a number of instances where Krause attempted to trade Pippen, only to have various reasons for not having the deal consummated in the end.

Even though he was part of the massive exodus at the end of the 1998 championship summer and lockout that followed, Pippen returned to appear in 23 games for the Bulls as a 38-year-old in the 2003–04 season before hanging up his sneakers.

Pippen still ranks second all-time among Bulls players in games played, minutes played, field goals, and field goal attempts—all behind only Jordan. He ranks fourth in team history in free throws, third in offensive rebounds, second in defensive rebounds, and third in total rebounds. And he trails only Jordan in assists and steals in franchise history.

JUNE 28
2006

Tyrus Thomas speaking at the draft

A BAD TRADE

AT THE START of the 2006 NBA Draft, the Chicago Bulls owned the No. 2 overall pick. They were once again looking to add an impact player to their lineup with a high draft pick; Chicago had selected in the top-three in 2001, 2002, and 2004, but needed to add athleticism inside.

That year's draft class had some interesting prospects, but nobody stood out as a franchise player. When the Bulls submitted their selection, it was Texas power forward LaMarcus Aldridge. But he wasn't the player Chicago was targeting.

During the draft, the Bulls traded Aldridge and a second-round pick to Portland for the No. 4 overall pick (forward Tyrus Thomas) and Viktor Khryapa.

Thomas was a dynamic forward who could fly above the rim. He had authored plenty of highlight-reel dunks in his freshman season at LSU, which appealed to the Bulls more than Aldridge's traditional post game.

Aldridge went on to appear in 1,076 regular-season games and appeared in the NBA All-Star Game seven times for the Blazers and Spurs during a solid NBA career.

Thomas, on the other hand, averaged 7.8 points per game over three-plus seasons for the Bulls and played in 402 career regular-season games.

JO

FANS REMEMBER THE 2007 NBA Draft mostly because the Portland Trail Blazers took Greg Oden instead of Kevin Durant with the first overall pick. But the ninth overall selection that year made a name for himself right away on draft night—and carried that vibe throughout a terrific career.

The Chicago Bulls were looking for energy in the paint, and they found it in Florida center Joakim Noah. The son of a tennis star, Noah arrived on the stage in a suit that became infamous immediately. His enormous, infectious smile was apparent at the draft.

Among players selected during the 2007 draft, Noah's career 9.0 rebound per game average ranks first. He was cut from the same cloth as Dennis Rodman, and he started his career with nine great seasons in Chicago.

His hustle up and down the floor made him one of Chicago's favorite players since Jordan left town. His jerseys were visible at every game, as was his trademark hair and smile. His shot may have been unorthodox, but his effort was undeniable. Noah was a force for the Bulls, especially on the defensive end of the floor.

Noah was named to the NBA's All-Defensive first team twice for the Bulls. He still ranks fourth in team history in total rebounds and third in blocked shots. His 1,910 offensive rebounds are the most in franchise history.

Though he finished his career with four injury-plagued seasons for the Knicks, Grizzlies, and Clippers, he remains a player many will forever associate with a fun, hard-working Chicago Bulls squad.

Noah in his iconic fit at the NBA Draft

D-ROSE COMES HOME

THE 2008 NBA Draft was historic for a number of reasons, and it started at the draft lottery. The Bulls only had a 1.7 percent chance of winning the lottery, but the ping pong balls landed in their favor. It was the second-biggest upset in NBA draft lottery history, and for only the second time in franchise history the Bulls would make the first pick in the draft.

There were some potential superstar players at the top of the draft class. UCLA teammates Russell Westbrook and Kevin Love, Kansas State's Michael Beasley, and USC's O. J. Mayo were strong candidates for the top pick. Indeed, there were a lot of analysts who felt Beasley was the top player in the draft.

But the Bulls had an easy choice. When the pick was submitted, they selected a dynamic point guard from their backyard. Derrick Rose had starred at Simeon Vocational Academy in Chicago during his remarkable high school career before leading Memphis to the Final Four. The local player was coming home.

Beasley and Mayo followed Rose off the board, making 2008 the first time in NBA history that freshmen were selected with the first three picks in the draft.

Number-one overall pick Derrick Rose with the commissioner.

Taj Gibson showing off his new Bulls jersey and number

TAJ

BEFORE THE 2009 NBA Trade Deadline, the Chicago Bulls traded guard Thabo Sefolosha to the Oklahoma City Thunder for a first-round pick. When the draft arrived, Chicago owned the 16th and 26th overall picks, with No. 26 coming from the trade with the Thunder.

At No. 16, the Bulls selected wing James Johnson from Wake Forest.

At No. 26, the Bulls selected forward Taj Gibson from USC.

Johnson would go on to have a modest NBA career, but Gibson emerged as a high-flying fan favorite in Chicago almost immediately. Gibson became a terrific defensive power forward for the Bulls and also had no problem living above the rim. He earned All-Rookie honors after his first season in the league.

However, maybe no play from his time in Chicago stands out more than Gibson dunking over Dwyane Wade during the 2011 NBA Playoffs. That clip will live forever online as one of the best posters in Bulls' history.

Over seven-plus seasons in Chicago, Gibson's numbers—9.4 points and 6.4 rebounds per game—don't stand out nearly as much as the love he had for the game or the love he received from the fans at the United Center.

2009

HOMEGROWN ROY

ON APRIL 22, 2009, for just the second time in the history of the franchise, a Bulls player was named the NBA Rookie of the Year alone (Elton Brand had shared the award). For the first time since Michael Jordan in 1985, the top freshman honor in the league was bestowed on a Chicago player—one who was born and raised in the city he now represented.

Derrick Rose received 111 of 120 first-place votes, becoming a nearly unanimous winner of the award. Memphis' O. J. Mayo was the runner-up, and New Jersey's Brook Lopez finished third. Rose was named the Eastern Conference Rookie of the Month three times (November, December, March), and he scored in double digits 71 times—including 32 games of at least 20 points. He appeared in 81 of 82 games, starting 80 times.

The first overall pick in the 2008 NBA Draft, Rose led first-year players in assists (6.3 per game) and was second among rookies in scoring (16.8 ppg). He finished the season in the top three in several categories all-time among Bulls rookies, including total points (third, with 1,361), scoring (third, with 16.8 points per game), and assists (third, with 6.3).

The Chicago kid was the goods from the get-go.

Kerr and Durham were the voices of Bulls basketball for a generation.

HONORING RED

IT REALLY DOESN'T matter what era of Bulls basketball you watched. There was one constant throughout the years: Johnny "Red" Kerr.

Kerr was the team's first head coach, and he later spent a brief time in the front office. In 1975, play-by-play announcer Jim Durham suggested Kerr would be a good fit on the home broadcasts of Bulls' games as a color commentator. From 1985 to 1991, Durham and Kerr worked together on radio and television broadcasts, capturing the early stages of Michael Jordan's incredible career and becoming the soundtrack to so many fans' Bulls experience.

He became part of Jordan's pre-game rituals as well. MJ would clap talcum powder in front of Kerr during warm-ups every night.

From 1975 until the end of the 2007–08 season, Kerr's voice was synonymous with the Chicago Bulls. Unfortunately, prostate cancer limited his availability for broadcasts moving forward, but he still made occasional appearances; he loved the Bulls and their fans almost as much as the fans and organization loved him.

On February 10, 2009, the Bulls honored Kerr's contributions to the franchise with a sculpture. You don't see many sculptures of broadcasters, but it was fitting that Kerr would have one in Chicago. That night also saw Jerry Colangelo present Kerr with the Naismith Memorial Basketball Hall of Fame's John W. Bunn Lifetime Achievement Award, and there were video messages from NBA Commissioner David Stern and other dignitaries, including Bulls fan and President of the United States Barack Obama.

MICHAEL JORDAN: HALL OF FAMER

On April 3, 2009, the Naismith Memorial Basketball Hall of Fame announced its induction class. Unfortunately for two members of that year's class, the ceremony would serve as a painful reminder of what wasn't.

Four members of the class had marvelous, distinguished careers. David Robinson and John Stockton were teammates on the Dream Team. Two coaches were among the members, including one whose career took off in Chicago. C. Vivian Stringer was joined by Bulls great Jerry Sloan.

For Sloan and Stockton, the fifth member of the induction class made the peaks of their respective careers a second-place finish.

That fifth member was Michael Jeffrey Jordan.

Jordan was obviously inducted in his first year of eligibility. His resume included an NCAA championship at North Carolina and two unanimous NCAA All-American honors. In the NBA, Jordan was a 14-time All-Star, 10-time scoring champion, three-time steals champion, 1984–85 Rookie of the Year, nine-time All-Defensive team, and 11-time All-NBA. He won six NBA championships and was the Finals MVP all six times. He was named the NBA MVP five times, was the 1987–88 Defensive Player of the Year, and was named the All-Star Game MVP three times.

"We have all known that it was only a matter of time before Springfield came calling. What Michael did for the Chicago Bulls, the city of Chicago, and the game of basketball can never be fully measured," Bulls Chairman Jerry Reinsdorf said in the team's statement following the announcement. "Michael Jordan is the greatest player to have ever played the game and on behalf of our entire organization, we congratulate him on this honor."

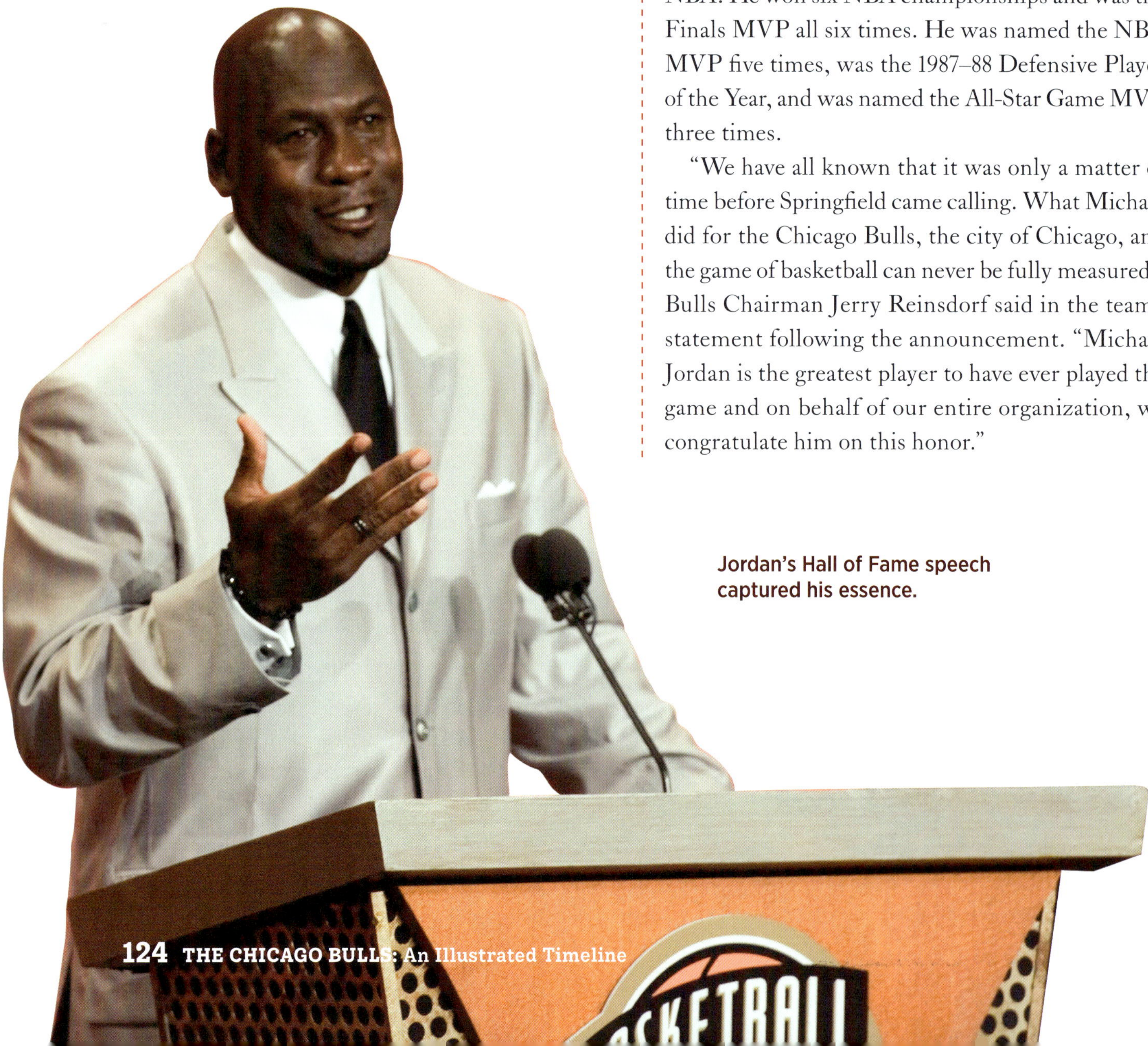

Jordan's Hall of Fame speech captured his essence.

SCOTTIE PIPPEN: HALL OF FAMER

WHEN THE NAISMITH Memorial Basketball Hall of Fame announced its induction class for 2010, the list of inducted honorees was longer than usual. Two entire teams—the 1960 USA Men's Olympic team and the 1992 "Dream Team"—were inducted together as groups.

Individually, the class included women's great Cynthia Cooper, Lakers owner Jerry Buss, famed New Jersey high school coach Bob Hurley Sr., and Karl Malone. In the Legends category, Dennis Johnson, Gus Johnson, and international star Maciel "Ubiratan" Pereira were inducted.

They were joined by Scottie Pippen, who celebrated both his personal induction and his induction as a member of the Dream Team.

"As an individual player, it's something I never could have dreamed," Pippen said in the Bulls' press release. "It's not an accolade that you can just go out and achieve. You have to impress people by the way you play the game. I tried to play the game the right way my whole career, played to win, and tried to be the best."

Pippen, like Michael Jordan the year before, was inducted in his first year of eligibility. He was a seven-time NBA All-Star and was All-NBA seven times as well. He was the 1994–95 steals champion and was named to the NBA's All-Defensive team 10 times. Pippen was named the 1994 NBA All-Star Game MVP and won six championships as a member of the Bulls.

Michael and Scottie together again

2010

BOOZER

ON JULY 8, 2010, the Bulls traded Mario Austin to the Utah Jazz for a second-round pick and power forward Carlos Boozer.

Boozer, who enjoyed a terrific career at Duke, was originally a second-round pick by the Cavs in 2002. He was named All-NBA after the 2007–08 season and was an NBA All-Star twice in Utah before the Jazz decided to move him to Chicago.

In four seasons with the Bulls, Boozer averaged 15.5 points and nine rebounds per game during the regular season.

In 2011, Boozer had a good run in the playoffs with the Bulls. He averaged a double-double in the first round against Indiana, a series the Bulls won in five games. His scoring increased to 13.3 points per game in a second-round win against the Hawks. His scoring went up again to 14.4 points, and he averaged 10.2 rebounds per game in the Eastern Conference Finals against Miami, a series the Bulls unfortunately lost in five games.

Boozer averaged a double-double in three of the seven postseason series in which he appeared with the Bulls.

Chicago waived Boozer in 2014, and he finished his career with the Lakers.

Boozer was a productive player in Chicago.

Butler soared during his time with the Bulls.

JIMMY BUCKETS

ON JUNE 23, 2011, the Chicago Bulls owned two picks in the first-round of the NBA draft. What wasn't considered in incredibly good or deep class was headlined by Duke guard Kyrie Irving, but after that there were lots of questions. Chicago's first pick came all the way down at No. 28 overall; their second was the last pick of the first round.

After 29 names were called—including Irving, Klay Thompson, Kawhi Leonard, and Nikola Vučević—the Bulls were on the clock for a second time. They selected Marquette guard Jimmy Butler.

More than a decade later, an argument can be made that Butler has been the most impactful player from that year's draft class.

Butler's fourth NBA season (2014–15) saw him appear in the All-Star Game for the first time. That season he was named the NBA's Most Improved Player.

In six seasons with the Bulls, Butler averaged 15.6 points per game. He represented Chicago in three NBA All-Star Games and saw his scoring average climb to almost 24 points per game in his final season with the team.

YOUNGEST MVP EVER

THE NBA FIRST handed out a Most Valuable Player Award at the end of the 1955–56 season. Since then, only two Chicago Bulls have won the award: Michael Jordan and Derrick Rose.

But no player has won the award at a younger age than Rose.

Before the 2010–11 season began, Rose asked the media why he couldn't win the MVP award that year. It would be just his third season in the league, but he already had the Rookie of the Year trophy at home and had shown that he was becoming one of the most dynamic guards in the league.

He answered his own question on the floor that season. Rose averaged 25 points and 7.7 assists per game in 81 appearances, leading the Bulls to a 62–20 record and first place in the Central Division. Rose led the team in scoring and assists, but was helped along the way by Carlos Boozer, Luol Deng, and Joakim Noah.

What made the award special for Bulls fans was that Rose was one of them. He was the local kid who made good. The former high school phenom in the Chicago Public League had grown into one of the best basketball players on the planet—and he was doing it in his hometown.

Rose was named the youngest MVP in NBA history; he was 22 years and 191 days old on the final day of the regular season. The mark was previously held by Wes Unseld, who in 1969 was 23 years and 9 days old when he won the award.

For many fans, hope that the Bulls would return to their championship-winning ways was poured into Rose. He represented so much to the city, and the applause when he was handed the MVP trophy was as loud as any for a Bulls game since 23 left the team.

The youngest to ever win the NBA's MVP Award

JUNE 2011

Coach Thibs's tough approach translated to wins in Chicago.

COACH THIBS

TOM THIBODEAU PAID his dues in the NBA. He served as an assistant coach in the league for 20 years, working in Minnesota, San Antonio, Philadelphia, Houston, and Boston, and with the New York Knicks. After all those years, it might have felt like his shot at becoming a head coach in the Association had passed.

But on June 23, 2010, the Bulls named Thibodeau their head coach. The 52-year-old finally got his chance.

In his first season on the bench in Chicago, Thibodeau was named the NBA's Coach of the Year. The Bulls were 62–20 that season and advanced to the Eastern Conference Finals. He was the Eastern Conference Coach of the Month three times that season.

In the three seasons that followed, the Bulls would win 50, 45, and 48 games, respectively. But only once in those three postseasons would the Bulls get out of the first round.

The Bulls fired Thibodeau on May 28, 2015, despite the team making the playoffs in every season in which he was the head coach. He was hired 11 months later by the Minnesota Timberwolves, and he won a second Coach of the Year award with the Knicks in 2021.

APRIL 28
2012

A heartbreaking moment for basketball fans

HEARTBREAK

"IT'S LIKE THE saddest win."

The Chicago Bulls had legitimate championship aspirations when they began the 2012 postseason. Even though superstar guard Derrick Rose was limited to 39 of the 66 games that season, Chicago finished 50–16 and in first place in the Central Division.

Rose had been hampered by a series of physical issues throughout the regular season: turf toe, back spasms, a pulled groin, and foot injuries. But he looked like himself in the first game of the Bulls' first round playoff series against the Philadelphia 76ers. He had 23 points, nine rebounds, and nine assists in a strong Game 1 victory; the Bulls won by 12.

But with 82 seconds left in the game, Rose tried to jump off his left foot in the lane and came down in pain. He had suffered a torn ACL. His postseason was over, as were the Bulls' chances of winning a title. Chicago was eliminated by Philly in six games.

It was guard Kyle Korver who said Game 1 was the saddest win. Many questioned why Rose was still in the game that late with the Bulls holding a commanding lead.

Unfortunately, the injury would cost Rose the entire following season as well. And it changed the trajectory of the franchise for the next decade.

Rose would come back as a 25-year-old for the 2013–14 season, but appear in only 10 games. In only two more years with the Bulls, Rose would appear in just 117 total games. He was traded to the Knicks before the 2016–17 season.

NOAH DEFENSIVE PLAYER OF THE YEAR

THE 2013–14 SEASON was the best of Joakim Noah's career. And the league recognized his effort with some individual accolades.

For the second time in as many seasons, Noah represented the Bulls in the NBA All-Star Game. He averaged career-highs in points (12.6), rebounds (11.3), and steals (1.2) that season, and he also averaged 1.5 blocked shots per night. Noah was the centerpiece of the Bulls' league-best defense; they allowed a league-low 91.8 points per game that season.

After Chicago finished second in the Central Division, a disappointing playoff exit in the first round did not keep Noah from receiving more recognition. He added All-NBA First Team and All-Defensive First Team honors to his resume. And he was named the NBA's Defensive Player of the Year.

Since the NBA started handing out a Defensive Player of the Year award in 1983, only two Bulls have won the hardware: Michael Jordan in 1988 and Noah in 2014. And since 2011, no player who has won the award has averaged more than Noah's 35.3 minutes per game that season.

Noah accepting his DPOY trophy from legend Dikembe Mutumbo

JULY 19
2014

BULLS LAND PAU

LOOKING TO ADD a quality big to their lineup in the summer of 2014, the Bulls turned to a player they missed on drafting in 2001—Pau Gasol. Gasol was coming off a marvelous tenure with the Lakers during which he had partnered with Kobe Bryant to make the Lakers successful for nearly a decade.

Gasol was 34 when he arrived in Chicago but was still an excellent player. He averaged 18.5 points and 11.8 rebounds per game in his first season for the Bulls and was named an NBA All-Star. He followed that performance with another All-Star caliber season, averaging 16.5 points and 11 rebounds per game.

He helped the Bulls return to the postseason in 2015, where the Bulls beat the Bucks in the first round with Gasol playing very well. Chicago lost to the Cleveland Cavaliers in the second round of the playoffs that season and failed to qualify for the postseason in 2016.

Gasol left as a free agent after only two seasons in Chicago.

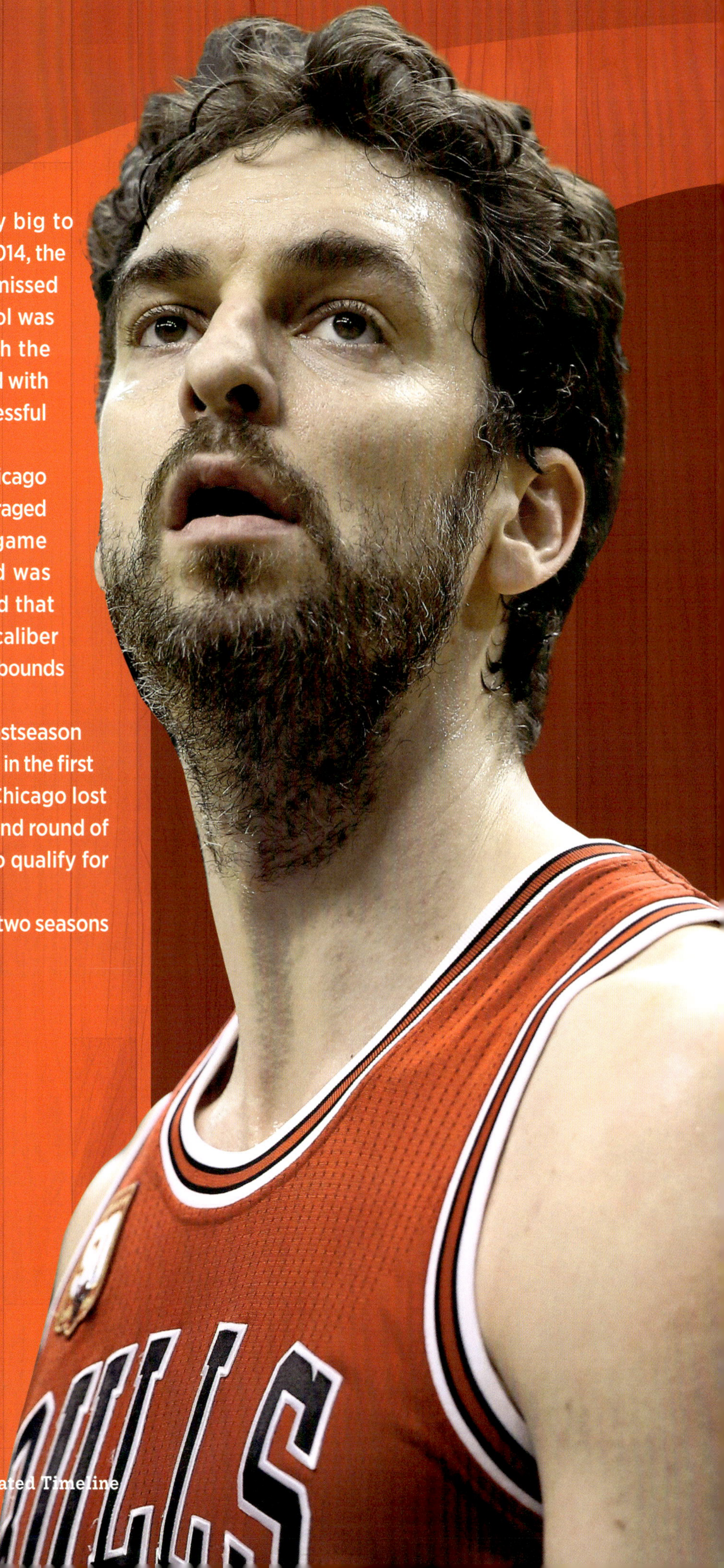

Gasol brought leadership and production to the Bulls.

JULY 15
2016

Richards High School legend Dwyane Wade came home.

D-WADE COMES HOME

ON JULY 15, 2016, the prodigal son returned . . . sort of. The Chicago Bulls turned the dreams of their fans into reality: Dwyane Wade was coming home.

Wade, who played high school ball at suburban Richards High School and went on to a stellar career at Marquette, was poached by the Miami Heat with the fifth pick in the 2005 NBA Draft—two spots before Chicago went on the clock. After 13 years, 12 NBA All-Star Games, and three championships with the Heat, Wade signed a multi-year deal to play for his hometown team.

Unfortunately, things did not play out in the storybook way many had hoped for. Wade averaged under 30 minutes per game for the first time in his career and appeared in only 60 games. His 18.3 point per game average was the lowest of his career since his rookie season. And after only one season back in Chicago, Wade was waived by the Bulls.

He received a hero's welcome and is still loved by many fans in Chicago. The timing for the player and franchise just weren't right for a homecoming.

COBY

ON JUNE 20, 2019, the NBA held its annual draft. The Chicago Bulls owned the seventh overall selection in a draft that was headlined by two potential superstars: Zion Williamson and Ja Morant. Those two went with the first two picks, to New Orleans and Memphis, respectively. When the Bulls were ready to make their pick, a point guard they needed was available.

Chicago selected North Carolina's Coby White.

White, with his enormous hair and a smile to match, had averaged 16.1 points per game in his one season for the Tar Heels, earning All-ACC and ACC All-Freshman honors.

He joined a Bulls roster that was in flux. The organization was still trying to figure out what to do with Lauri Markkanen and Wendell Carter, Jr. They had acquired Zach LaVine, but weren't happy with the combination of Kris Dunn and Ryan Arcidiacono at point guard.

White averaged 13.2 points per game and earned NBA All-Rookie Team recognition as a 19-year-old in his first full professional season. In the seasons that followed, White's production was up and down as the Bulls added veteran Lonzo Ball.

He emerged as a bona fide Most Improved Player candidate during the 2023–24 season campaign with a breakout season, averaging almost 20 points per game and establishing career bests in assists (5.2 per game), rebounds (4.7 per game), and minutes (36.6 per game). He also showed that he could make clutch shots in big moments.

White's hat didn't fit as well as he did in the Bulls' rotation.

BUTLER FOR LAVINE

ON JUNE 22, 2017, the Chicago Bulls consummated a controversial trade. Chicago sent Jimmy Butler to the Minnesota Timberwolves for guards Zach LaVine and Kris Dunn and forward Lauri Markkanen.

In six seasons with the Bulls after he was the 30th overall pick in the 2011 NBA Draft, Butler had been a good player. He averaged 15.6 points per game in 399 contests for the Bulls, but he was at odds with the front office about the future of the team. So, they moved him out for a package of high-end talent.

Markkanen was a seven-foot player who was the seventh overall pick in the 2017 NBA Draft. The Bulls were high on Dunn's leadership as a point guard. But the wild card in the deal was LaVine, who was a Slam Dunk Contest champion who could fly out of the gym but hadn't shown the ability to elevate his game in the NBA—yet.

Dunn never materialized as a viable NBA guard. And even though Markkanen made the 2017–18 All-Rookie Team, the Bulls moved on from the seven-footer after four seasons. LaVine was given a more prominent role in Chicago and took advantage, becoming one of the more lethal scorers in the league.

LaVine lived above the rim, producing highlight-worthy dunks.

THE 2020 ALL-STAR GAME

ON FEBRUARY 16, 2020, the Chicago Bulls hosted the NBA All-Star Game. The game served as a way for the NBA to come together and remember the accomplishments on and off the court of Lakers legend Kobe Bryant, who had tragically died in an accident three weeks before the game took place. The NBA named the All-Star Game MVP Award for Bryant during the event.

What we didn't know at that time was this event would come less than one month before the sports world shut down because of the COVID-19 pandemic. During the events, the Bulls had a few players participating.

Chicago was represented by forward Wendell Carter Jr. in the Rising Stars Challenge. Team USA beat Team World 151–131 in the game. Miami forward Bam Adebayo defeated Domantas Sabonis in the final of the Skills Competition.

Buddy Hield defeated Devin Booker to win the Three Point Contest. Bulls guard Zach LaVine finished fourth on the competition. And Heat guard Derrick Jones Jr., who would later play for the Bulls, upset Orlando's Aaron Gordon in the Slam Dunk Contest.

The game itself had a pick-up game player draft format. Milwaukee's Giannis Antetokounmpo and Lakers star LeBron James were the team captains. The Bulls did not have a representative in the game, unfortunately. Team LeBron beat Team Giannis 157–155, and Kawhi Leonard was named the NBA All-Star Game Kobe Bryant MVP.

The NBA brought the All-Star Game back to Chicago.

NBA ALL-STAR 2020
CHICAGO
NBA ALL-STAR 2020
CHICAGO
PERIOD 2
FOUL
FOUL
BULLS
5:30
27
TOL 5/0

APRIL 13
2020

NEW LEADERSHIP

AFTER A DISTINGUISHED professional career in Europe and the Olympics on behalf of Lithuania, Arturas Karnišovas made the move to North America to work in basketball operations. Beginning in 2003, he spent five years in the NBA's league office before becoming an international scout for the Houston Rockets.

Karnišovas joined the Denver Nuggets' front office as their assistant general manager in 2013. When he became a hot name for other openings around the league, the Nuggets promoted him to their GM job in 2017.

His resume was impressive in Denver, but postseason success didn't come as quickly as he wanted. When the Chicago Bulls offered him the role of executive vice president of basketball operations in April of 2020, he accepted.

Under the leadership of Karnišovas, the Bulls hired Marc Eversley as the permanent general manager. Eversley is the first person of color to serve as the Bulls' GM. Eversley is also the first Canadian-trained basketball player to become an NBA general manager.

Karnišovas represented a new era of leadership for the Bulls.

2020

Donovan brought a track record of success to Chicago.

A NEW HEAD COACH

ON SEPTEMBER 22, 2020, the Bulls made a bold hire for their new head coach. After five successful seasons in Oklahoma City—in which the Thunder made the playoffs all five years—Billy Donovan was coming to Chicago.

Donovan had coached Bulls' legend Joakim Noah to great success at the University of Florida before making the jump to the NBA. He guided the Thunder to the NBA Finals in 2016, his first season as an NBA head coach.

His first season in Chicago didn't go as well as planned, with the Bulls winning just 31 games. But Donovan was back in the postseason the next year; the Bulls won 46 regular-season games but were eliminated in the first round of the playoffs in 2022.

MARCH 2021

Vučević became the man in the middle for the Bulls.

VOOCH

ON MARCH 25, 2021, the Bulls consummated one of the biggest trades in the history of the franchise. Chicago sent Wendell Carter Jr., Otto Porter Jr., and first-round picks in 2021 and 2023 to the Orlando Magic for Al-Farouq Aminu and center Nikola Vučević.

Vučević, 30 at the time of the trade, was considered one of the better centers in the NBA. He had appeared in four NBA All-Star Games with the Magic and, at the time of the deal, was averaging 24.5 points and 11.8 rebounds per game.

In his first two seasons with the Bulls, Vučević averaged 17.6 points per game and 11 rebounds.

On June 28, 2023, the Bulls agreed to a three-year, $60 million extension with Vučević.

JULY 29

2021

MORGAN PARK REPRESENT

THE SUMMER OF 2021 was a tumultuous one for the Chicago Bulls. Chicago was one of the more active teams in the trade market, making big-time sign-and-trade deals for Lonzo Ball and DeMar DeRozan and sending Lauri Markkanen to Cleveland. At the trade deadline during the 2020–21 season, the Bulls sent their first-round pick (No. 8 overall) to the Orlando Magic in a blockbuster trade that brought center Nikola Vučević to Chicago.

It was going to be a whole new look on the court for the Chicago Bulls.

But the trades had stripped the roster of a lot of its depth. And Chicago still needed to have impact players available to support their new crew of stars.

Chicago only had one pick in the 2021 NBA Draft, a second-round pick they acquired from New Orleans in a trade in 2018 that sent Nikola Mirotic to the Pelicans.

With the 40th overall pick in the 2021 NBA Draft, the Chicago Bulls selected guard Ayo Dosunmu.

Dosunmu, known for his hair and defense, was a Chicago guy—he played at Morgan Park High School before spending three years leading the Fighting Illini at the University of Illinois. He had been a consensus All-American as a junior for the Illini, averaging better than 20 points per game.

Ayo was named to the NBA's All-Rookie team following the 2021–22 season and saw his role grow in the seasons that followed as injuries kept Ball from being available.

Dosunmu became another local kid to wear the Bulls jersey in the NBA.

JANUARY 1
2021

DEMAR DE MAN

ON AUGUST 11, 2021, the Bulls negotiated a sign-and-trade deal with the San Antonio Spurs that brought veteran wing DeMar DeRozan to Chicago.

In his first season with the Bulls, DeRozan was named second team All-NBA. His 27.9 points per game were not only a career best but ranked fifth in the entire NBA. And he was as clutch as it gets. On New Year's Eve, DeRozan hit a game-winning three at the buzzer to give the Bulls a 108–106 win in Indiana. The following day—New Year's Day—he hit another game-winning three at the buzzer to give the Bulls a 120–119 win in Washington. He became the first player in NBA history with a game-winning buzzer-beater on consecutive days.

Later that first season in Chicago, DeRozan set an NBA record by scoring at least 35 points while shooting 50 percent or better in eight consecutive games. The king of the mid-range game was thought to be washed up when the Bulls acquired him, but he was soon playing the best ball of his career.

DeRozan represented the Bulls in the NBA All-Star Game in each of his first two seasons and became a veteran leader on the team.

DeRozan flashing his legendary midrange game

FEBRUARY 20

2022

The Bulls were well represented among the NBA's all-time greats.

NBA'S 75TH ANNIVERSARY TEAM

DURING THE 2021–22 season, the NBA put together a group of current and former NBA players, coaches, general managers, and team and league executives, along with WNBA legends, sportswriters, and broadcasters to create the league's 75th Anniversary Team. A group of 76 players ranging from the infancy of the league to the current day were selected.

The Chicago Bulls were well represented. Though I won't include Carmelo Anthony as a "one-time Bulls player" on the list, there was still a strong collection of Bulls players who were chosen.

Michael Jordan and Scottie Pippen are best remembered as Chicago Bulls. But Robert Parrish, Dennis Rodman, Nate Thurmond, and Dwyane Wade also spent time in Chicago and made the list as well.

Jordan, Pippen, former Bull Steve Kerr, Naperville native Candace Parker, former Bulls coach Doug Collins, and Chicagoan Jerry Colangelo were among the panelists tasked with putting together the list. Though current and former players were not able to vote for themselves, Jordan and Pippen had no trouble making the cut.

The full roster was introduced at the 2022 NBA All-Star Game.

LaVine skying for another signature throw-down

HIGH RISER

When the Bulls acquired Zach LaVine from Minnesota, he was primarily known as a ferocious dunker with ridiculous hops. But there had been some frustration from Timberwolves fans that his overall offensive toolkit hadn't lived up to the production they had seen while he was playing at UCLA.

He answered all those questions with a more significant opportunity in Chicago. On June 22, 2017, the Bulls consummated a somewhat controversial trade. Jimmy Butler and the 16th overall pick in the 2022 NBA Draft were sent to Minnesota for LaVine, guard Kris Dunn, and the 7th overall pick in the 2022 NBA Draft. The Bulls selected forward Lauri Markkanen with the seventh overall selection.

LaVine's scoring average dipped to 16.7 in just 24 games in his first season with the Bulls, but he has averaged at least 23.7 points per game in each season since. He posted a career-best 27.4 during the 2020–21 season before the pandemic shut down the NBA.

LaVine represented the Bulls in the NBA All-Star Game for the first time that season; he returned the following year.

On April 9, 2021, LaVine erupted for the first 50-point game of his career. He hit 7 of 12 from beyond the arc and 18 of 31 shots overall for an even 50 points in 38:44 on the floor. Unfortunately, the milestone performance came in a losing effort; the Bulls fell 120–108 in Atlanta.

On October 28, 2023, LaVine set another new career high. He scored 51 points—20 of which came in the third quarter. His numbers were incredibly similar to his first 50-point night: LaVine hit 7 of 13 from three-point range and 19 of 33 overall in 37:26 in the game. And, unfortunately once again, he did it in a road loss. The Bulls fell 118–102 in Detroit that night.

LaVine's two 50-point games are tied with the man for whom he was traded, Jimmy Butler, for the second-most in Bulls' franchise history; Michael Jordan reached that total 30 times. Jordan, LaVine, and Butler are the only three players to have more than one 50-point game in the history of the team.

Though he was best known for highlights he created above the rim, LaVine established himself as the most prolific three-point shooter in the history of the Bulls before his time in Chicago came to an end.

Ben Gordon had the Bulls' record for three-pointers made in a season with 173 in 2008–09 before LaVine arrived. LaVine eclipsed that number, hitting 184 in the 2019–20 season. And he was only getting started with the franchise's leaderboard. LaVine would hit an even 200 from deep in the 2020–21 season and 185 more during the 2021–22 campaign.

LaVine broke the Bulls' franchise record for three-pointers made in a single season on April 4, 2023—a record he had set. He finished the 2022–23 season with 204 three-pointers made. That number has since been passed twice by Coby White, but LaVine owns two of four seasons in Bulls' history in which a player hit at least 200 three-pointers. LaVine owns four of the six most prolific three-point seasons in club history.

As of the end of the 2024–25 season, only two players in Bulls history had made more than 1,000 three-pointers with the team: LaVine (1,130) and Kirk Hinrich (1,049). LaVine also owns the most three-point attempts (2,898) in team history. And, impressively, LaVine made 39 percent of those attempts during his time with the Bulls.

The Bulls honored their all-time best in 2023.

RING OF HONOR

ON DECEMBER 12, 2023, the Chicago Bulls introduced a new way to celebrate the incredible history of the franchise: the Chicago Bulls Ring of Honor.

The Bulls displayed unique artifacts from the various honorees in lockers around the United Center Atrium in the days before the Bulls hosted the Golden State Warriors on January 12, and the team hosted a private gala for the honorees and other guests the night before that game.

Why the Golden State Warriors? Because their coach, Steve Kerr, was a member of the 1995–96 Bulls team that had the best regular-season record in the history of the NBA up to that point, 72–10, and won the 1996 NBA Championship. That entire team was part of the inaugural induction class, which also included 13 individual Bulls legends.

The individuals who were part of the first class in the Ring of Honor: Artis Gilmore, Phil Jackson, Michael Jordan, Johnny "Red" Kerr, Dick Klein, Jerry Krause, Toni Kukoč, Bob Love, Scottie Pippen, Dennis Rodman, Jerry Sloan, Chet Walker, and Tex Winter.

"The Chicago Bulls Ring of Honor will be a first-of-its-kind celebration honoring many of the legends who have helped shaped our organization over the past 57 years," Michael Reinsdorf, president and chief executive officer, said in the team's press release. "They have deep connections to our fans and community and represent a spirit of competition, hard work, and toughness. This January, we look forward to cementing their legacy in Bulls history and inspiring the future of our organization."

The individuals who were part of the first class in the Bulls' Ring of Honor: Artis Gilmore, Phil Jackson, Michael Jordan, Johnny "Red" Kerr, Dick Klein, Jerry Krause, Toni Kukoč, Bob Love, Scottie Pippen, Dennis Rodman, Jerry Sloan, Chet Walker, and Tex Winter.

1995–96 Chicago Bulls

Players: Randy Brown, Jud Buechler Jason Caffey, James Edwards, Jack Haley, Ron Harper, Michael Jordan, Steve Kerr, Toni Kukoč, Luc Longley, Scottie Pippen, Dennis Rodman, John Salley, Dickey Simpkins, and Bill Wennington

Coaches: Jim Cleamons, Phil Jackson, John Paxson, Jimmy Rodgers, and Tex Winter

Front Office Members: Ivica Dukan, Clarence Gaines Jr., Erik Heiland, Jerry Krause, John Ligmanowski, Chip Schaefer, Jim Stack, and Al Vermeil

JULY 8
2024

DEROZAN DEALT

DURING THE SUMMER following the 2023–24 season, the Chicago Bulls found themselves at a crossroads as a franchise. Some of their veterans were looking for new contracts, and some of their younger players had stepped up in recent seasons to earn more significant roles on the team.

The biggest decision the Bulls made came on July 8, 2024, when the Bulls made a trade that sent a fan favorite out of town. The three-team, sign-and-trade deal including the Sacramento Kings and San Antonio Spurs sent DeMar DeRozan to Sacramento.

DeRozan had spent only three years in Chicago, but he frequently showed why he is respected around the league. He represented the Bulls in the NBA All-Star Game in each of his first two seasons and led the league in minutes played per game in his third. He finished in the top three in voting for the Clutch Player of the Year Award (the Jerry West Trophy) twice and in the top ten for the league's most valuable player once.

He appeared in 229 games for the Bulls (all starts) and averaged 25.5 points, 4.7 rebounds, 5.1 assists, and 1.1 steals over his three campaigns in Chicago. When he was traded, DeRozan ranked second all-time in Bulls history in scoring average (25.5 ppg) and seventh in assists per game (5.1).

The Bulls received guard Chris Duarte, two second-round draft picks, and cash considerations in the three-team trade.

"We thank DeMar for everything he has done for our team as a leader and mentor," Bulls Executive Vice President of Basketball Operations Artūras Karnišovas said in the team's press release announcing the trade. "Everyone inside our building appreciated and respected DeMar's professionalism and commitment to this organization and the city of Chicago, and we wish him the best in Sacramento."

DeRozan left his mark during his time with the Bulls.

SACRAMENTO
KINGS
10
BULLS
4

BULLS
15
SACRAMENTO
KINGS
8

FEBRUARY 2

2025

LAVINE LEAVES

AFTER MOVING ON from DeMar DeRozan during the summer before the 2024–25 season, there was one veteran on the Bulls' roster whose future was in limbo. Zach LaVine had been a human highlight reel since coming to Chicago, but trade rumors had swirled around him over the last couple of seasons.

On February 2, 2025, that trade finally came. And, once again, it was a three-team deal that involved the same two teams as the DeRozan trade. And, ironically, this trade meant the one player who was acquired in the DeRozan trade no longer had a roster spot—and brought a draft pick back to Chicago that it had initially traded to get DeRozan in the first place.

The Bulls received Kevin Huerter from Sacramento as well as Zach Collins and Tre Jones from San Antonio in a blockbuster trade that also saw star guard De'Aaron Fox traded to the Spurs. The Bulls received their first-round pick in the 2025 NBA Draft back from the Spurs in the deal; they had traded that to San Antonio for DeRozan.

As a result of the three players added to the roster, the Bulls waived Chris Duarte. He was the player Chicago received when they traded DeRozan to Sacramento. Now LaVine would join his former Bulls teammate on the Kings' roster.

"Zach has been a cornerstone for this organization and the city," Bulls Executive Vice President of Basketball Operations Artūras Karnišovas said in the team's release announcing the trade. "He truly embraced what it means to be a Bull. His work ethic and passion for the game have been inspiring. During his time here, he not only grew as a player but also started a family, and we watched him develop into the person he is today."

LaVine appeared in 416 games (413 starts) over eight seasons in Chicago during which he averaged 24.2 points, 4.7 rebounds, 4.3 assists, and 0.9 steals in 34.5 minutes. When he was traded, LaVine ranked as the Bulls' all-time three-pointer leader (1,130). He also left town ranked third all-time in scoring average (behind Michael Jordan and DeRozan), sixth in total points (10,056), seventh in field goals made (3,545), and 12th in total assists (1,808) in Bulls history.

LaVine joined DeRozan in Sacramento.

BULLS
0

COBY EMERGES

WITH THE SEVENTH overall pick in the 2019 NBA Draft, the Chicago Bulls selected guard Coby White out of North Carolina. His draft night interviews went viral after the draft because of his excitement as some of his Tar Heel teammates were selected. That wouldn't be the end of White making headlines with the Bulls.

White was voted to the NBA's All-Rookie Second Team following a strong first professional season in which he averaged 13.2 points per game in 65 contests, mostly off the bench. Because of injuries, he found himself in the starting lineup 54 times in 69 appearances as a sophomore in the Association and increased his scoring to better than 15 points per game.

The next two years saw a lot of changes to the Bulls' lineup, and White was relegated back to a bench role. But the 2023–24 season saw him establish himself as an every-night starter for the Bulls.

White's scoring increased to 19.1 points per game in 78 starts that season. He also posted career-high averages in assists (5.1) and rebounds (4.5). His speed was evident every night, and he became a dangerous outside shooter as well.

He became an all-star candidate in his sixth NBA season in 2024–25, raising his scoring average to over 20 points per game. He was named the Eastern Conference Player of the Week twice in March and earned the conference's Player of the Month honors. The former McDonald's All-American started to get the ball in clutch moments as well. He posted a career-high 44 points at Orlando on March 6, two nights after he tied his previous career-best of 37. He scored at least 35 points in a game four times in March 2025.

White became a leader in the box score and on the court.

BULLS
14

LIL BUZI VERT

THE START OF the 2024 NBA Draft made history as Zaccharie Risacher and Alex Sarr heard their names called first (to Atlanta) and second (to Washington), respectively, at the top of the draft. Risacher followed Victor Wembanyama as the second consecutive first-overall selection from France. When Tidjane Salaun went sixth to Charlotte, it marked the first time in league history that three of the top 10 picks came from a non-US country.

The run on international players meant more US-born players were sliding down the board. And the Chicago Bulls, who began the 2024 NBA Draft with the 11th overall pick in the first round, were watching with optimism.

When their pick came up on the board, Chicago had one name to call. And it led to an emotional moment during the draft.

Matas Buzelis had grown up outside Chicago and started his high school career at Hinsdale Central High School in the western suburbs. His younger brother was still playing basketball for the Red Devils. He was a Bulls fan as a kid. And this was a homecoming that brought the prospect to tears during the broadcast of the draft.

Buzelis, a six-foot-ten-inch small forward with good handles and a chip on his shoulder, had played one season for the G League Ignite before the draft. Falling to the Bulls felt like a lottery ticket had cashed; he was considered one of the top prospects in the class.

Over the course of his rookie season, Buzelis got his hometown's fans on their feet regularly at the United Center. He represented the Bulls in the 2025 Slam Dunk Contest and posted five games with at least 20 points scored. Buzelis scored a rookie season-high 21 at the Lakers on March 22 and registered his first career double-double on April 4 against the Trail Blazers.

Buzelis earned All-Rookie Second Team recognition after averaging 8.6 points and 3.5 rebounds per game.

"The Hinsdale Hammer" is the future in Chicago.

APRIL 5
2025

DONOVAN TO THE HALL

ON APRIL 5, 2025, Chicago Bulls head coach Billy Donovan was named as part of the induction class for the Naismith Memorial Basketball Hall of Fame.

Donovan established himself as a coach during his tenure at the University of Florida, where he coached the Gators for 19 seasons (1996–2015). He led Florida to back-to-back NCAA championships with a roster that included future Chicago center Joakim Noah. He also led the Gators to four Final Fours, six SEC regular-season championships, and four SEC Tournament championships. Donovan led the Gators to 467 total wins.

At the NBA level, Donovan spent five seasons with the Oklahoma City Thunder (2015–20) before being named the head coach of the Bulls in 2020. At the time of his induction, Donovan had spent five years with the Bulls. His teams had a 243–157 record in Oklahoma City and, as of the end of the 2024–25 season, 195–205 in Chicago.

He was named the National Basketball Coaches Association Coach of the Year following his final season in Oklahoma City and has been named an NBA Coach of the Month twice, once in Oklahoma City (December 2019) and once in Chicago (November 2021).

"Billy's enshrinement into the Basketball Hall of Fame is a testament to a lifetime spent giving everything to the game," Chicago Bulls Chairman Jerry Reinsdorf said in the team's statement following the announcement. "It goes beyond his incredible success as a coach—it's about the relationships he's built, the players he's mentored, and the countless lives he's touched along the way. Billy has a remarkable basketball mind, but what truly sets him apart is who he is as a person. He leads with humility, heart, and a genuine care for everyone around him. Whether it's his players, his staff, or our community, he always puts others first. We're incredibly proud to have him as part of the Bulls family, and on behalf of the entire organization, I want to congratulate him on this well-earned and well-deserved honor."

Donovan was joined in the 2025 induction class by Carmelo Anthony, Micky Arison, Sue Bird, Danny Crawford, Sylvia Fowles, Dwight Howard, Maya Moore, and the 2008 US Men's Olympic Basketball Team.

He is the third former Bulls coach to be inducted into the Naismith Memorial Basketball Hall of Fame, joining Phil Jackson and Jerry Sloan. Former Bulls coach Doug Collins was inducted in 2024 as a contributor.

Donovan joins the greatest coaches in history.

2025

DRAFT LOTTERY LOSS LANDS NOA ESSENGUE

REMEMBER BACK IN 1979 when a literal coin toss cost the Chicago Bulls the opportunity to draft a generational superstar first overall in the NBA draft?

The 2024–25 Bulls were chasing a play-in tournament berth late in the regular season and got hot late. Starting on March 20, the Bulls put together win streaks of four, three and three games, respectively as they won 10 of their last 14 games to get in. The biggest win in that period was a stunning 146–115 win over the Lakers in Los Angeles on March 22.

At the same time, the Dallas Mavericks were falling apart at the seams and surrounded by turmoil. On February 2, in one of the most shocking blockbuster trades in the history of the NBA, the Mavs sent superstar guard Luka Dončić to the Lakers in a massive deal that, most notably, moved Anthony Davis back to Dallas. The three-team deal caught the entire sports world by surprise when the reports broke in the middle of the night.

Dallas lost five of their last seven games and limped—literally—into the play-in tournament. Davis had physical issues after the trade and they were without Kyrie Irving because of an injury as well. Fans in Dallas were calling for their general manager, Nico Harrison to be fired.

When the dust settled at the end of the regular season, the Bulls and Mavericks had identical 39-43 records.

To break the tie between the Bulls and Mavericks—and other teams in other slots in the NBA Draft Lottery order—the NBA conducted random drawings on April 21. The league announced the Mavericks won the drawing with the Bulls and were awarded the 11th-best odds of winning the 2025 NBA Draft Lottery. The Bulls would have the 12th-best odds of winning.

The prize in the 2025 NBA Draft was Duke forward Cooper Flagg, who was one of the best regarded prospects in recent years. He dominated the NCAA ranks in his one collegiate season and NBA teams had circled and looked forward to his draft year while he was still in high school.

On May 13, the 2025 NBA Draft Lottery took place in Chicago. The Mavericks had a 1.8 percent chance of winning the lottery, but the ping pong balls found the number combination that gave them the top pick in the draft. The Mavs became the 4th-largest underdog in the history of the NBA to win a draft lottery.

The Bulls, meanwhile, remained with the 12th overall pick.

When the 2025 NBA Draft began on June 26, the Mavericks triumphantly selected Flagg with the first overall selection.

The Chicago Bulls selected forward Noa Essengue with their pick.

Essengue, a 6-foot-9 stretch forward from France, had been playing professionally in Germany for a couple seasons before being eligible for the NBA Draft.

The following night when the NBA concluded its draft with the second round, the Bulls selected forward Lachlan Olbrich with a pick they acquired from the Lakers. Olbrich, who was 21 at the time, had been playing professionally in his native Australia.

French forward Noa Essengue becomes a Chicago Bull.

BULLS
ATLANTA
CHICAGO
BULLS
1
RENCY EXCHANGE
cinkciarz.pl

INDEX

Bob Love is one of the most beloved players in Bulls history.